The Tribulation

Part II
of a Trilogy

by

Dr. James H. Correll II

K&W, Inc.
3720 Flowood Drive
Jackson, Mississippi 39208

For Worldwide Distribution
Printed in the United States of America

ISBN - #0-9660647-1-2

Original design by Chad Tyler

Publication Supervisor: Donna Passmore

Contents

Introduction

There has always been much speculation about the Great Tribulation. Who is Antichrist and his False Prophet? What about the mark of the beast? Would God really pour out his wrath upon the earth, or are the judgments just symbolic? Perhaps the Apostle John had a really bad dream after eating some Mexican food!

I believe God wanted us to know the truth. I believe he wanted us to know that he is holy and unalterably opposed to sin; therefore, he must judge. I believe he wanted us to see the glorified Christ directing events from Heaven in the Great Tribulation. Jesus is the Lion.

Reading this book will make you a better witness, if you are a Christian. It will drive you to Christ, if you are not. This is God's Word about what will happen on earth after the church is raptured.

Many thanks to Donna Passmore, who gave me guidance throughout this project, and to my wife, Dianne, who patiently offered suggestions and proofreading assistance.

May our Lord bless you as you read this second part of the Revelation trilogy.

1

THE FIRST SIX SEALS

Revelation 6:1-17

Tribulation.

Great Tribulation.

The Great Tribulation.

The four horsemen of the Apocalypse.

The mark of the beast.

Armageddon.

You might think we are in tribulation now. Perhaps, but we are not in the Great Tribulation.

You might argue that a good God would not judge a wicked earth as described in Revelation. I contend a holy God must.

The Revelation of Jesus Christ unveils him as he really is. It is easy for us to accept him as a baby in a manger, as a Savior dying on a cross, even as a victor over the grave. But a holy judge, full of wrath? Somehow that doesn't fit our profile of him.

Wouldn't it be great to rest for awhile in the holiness of Heaven as seen in the fourth chapter of Revelation? I could spend eternity in the glory and worship of Christ as seen in Chapter 5. While we would like to remain on the mountaintop of those manifestations, we must also accept that Chapters 6-18 are part of the Revelation. We have to see the Great Tribulation upon the earth before we see Jesus Christ coming in power and glory in Chapter 19. The Great Tribulation period disturbs a lot of people, because they refuse to believe that Jesus Christ can be the harsh judge portrayed here.

What happens to the earth when the church leaves? While we are honoring, praising, and worshipping our Lord Jesus Christ in Heaven, what will those who are left behind be doing? The answer is frightening to consider.

The true church, as light and salt, will be gone from the earth during the Great Tribulation. From this point in the Book of Revelation, the church is no longer mentioned on the earth at all. The church will not be on the earth until it returns with Christ in power and glory. The Holy Spirit will restrain evil no longer. The Devil will know he has but a short time. Evil men will be free to carry out their awful plans.

There will be direct judgment from God carried out by Jesus Christ, the Lamb of God and the Lion of the tribe of Judah. Jesus is the Creator and Redeemer, and he is the only one worthy to judge and rule this earth. Those who will not accept Jesus as the Lamb of God must face him as the Lion and the Judge of God.

Opening of the Seven-Sealed Book (6:1)

In Chapter 5, John wept because no one was found who was worthy to open the book. The elder instructed him to stop crying and to direct his attention to the Lion of the tribe of Judah. When John looked, he saw a Lamb "as it had been slain" (Revelation 5:6), but it was standing. What he saw, of course, was the Lamb of God, Jesus Christ, who died as a sacrifice, but who also stands resurrected. The

Lamb took the book, and the hallelujah chorus began throughout all creation.

The Lamb opens the seals

And I saw when the Lamb opened one of the seals, and I heard, as it were the noise of thunder, one of the four beasts saying, Come and see (6:1).

Breaking the seven seals opens up the Great Tribulation period. Jesus breaks the seals, and the four horsemen ride forth.

The Great Tribulation is very orderly:
1. The seventh seal introduces the seven trumpets.
2. The seventh trumpet introduces seven persons.
3. The beast introduces the seven vials of wrath.
4. The seventh vial brings Babylon's judgment —
   Babylon represents political and religious
   rebellion against God.

If you don't remember anything else, remember this: the Great Tribulation is triggered from Heaven. It is directed from Heaven. The Lord Jesus Christ is the director. He possesses the book which the prophet Daniel sealed six or seven hundred years before the first advent and which is undoubtedly the title deed to the earth. Because he shed his blood to redeem mankind, the Lord Jesus Christ is worthy to own the book and to direct the judgments against the unrepentant earth.

Purposes of the judgments

What are the purposes of this Great Tribulation period? Why must the earth be judged?

The first purpose is to prepare Israel for her Messiah. John the Baptist prepared her for the first advent, and

Elijah will prepare her for the second:

> *Behold, I will send you Elijah the prophet before the coming of the great and dreadful day of the Lord: and he shall turn the heart of the fathers to the children, and the heart of the children to their fathers, lest I come and smite the earth with a curse (Mal 4:5-6).*

What is the day of the Lord? It is that period of time that starts immediately after the Rapture of the church. The next thing to happen on the prophetic calendar is the Rapture of the church. Nothing precludes that except the completion of the bride of Christ, and we do not know when that will happen. It could be today. The day of the Lord begins with the Rapture and ends with the Great White Throne judgment. The Great Tribulation period is at the beginning of this day of the Lord, which lasts at least 1,007 years.

Elijah is the one who will be sent before the day of the Lord. He will be one of two witnesses who will come during the Great Tribulation. We do not know who the other one is, and all our speculation will be fruitless. Some say Moses, others John the Baptist, or Enoch. The truth is, we have no idea, but we know Elijah will prepare Israel for the Second Coming of the Lord.

A multitude of Jews will be saved to populate the earth during the millennium. When Jesus returns to the earth in power and glory at the end of the Tribulation, he will establish his kingdom to rule and reign from the throne of David in Jerusalem for 1,000 years.

Christ will reign in peace during the millennium. Many have tried to establish peace in Israel. All have failed. The Antichrist will promise peace. He, too, will fail. Only the

Prince of Peace, the Lord Jesus Christ, will ever be able to bring lasting peace to the Middle East and the world.

The primary purpose, then, of this time of "Jacob's trouble" is to purge the nation Israel and to prepare her for the millennium.

The second purpose is to pour out judgment on unbelieving people. Godlessness, blasphemy, beast worship, false teaching, and unrepentance will be judged. The judgments are deliberate, successive, and of increasing intensity. Though they begin as rather mild and slow, they become worse and worse and come faster and faster. The first five seals occur over a period of three and one-half years. That's relatively slow. But the last three and one-half years of the Tribulation are characterized by one devastating plague after another, each worse than the last.

Four Horsemen of the Apocalypse (6:1-8)

The white horse rider: Antichrist (6:1-2)

And I saw, when the Lamb opened one of the seals, and I heard, as it were the noise of thunder, one of the four beasts saying, Come and see. And I saw, and behold a white horse: and he that sat on him had a bow; and a crown was given unto him: and he went forth conquering, and to conquer (6:1-2).

The noise of thunder signals a coming storm. When you hear thunder, you know that a storm is approaching. When John heard the noise of thunder, he knew a storm was brewing.

This white horse rider who gallops forth to the noise of the storm is not Christ, but Antichrist, imitator of Christ. He comes, not as a villain, but promising world unity and peace – he carries a bow, but no arrows. An empty bow is a promise of peace.   The world wants peace and economic stability, and the Antichrist will promise both.

Economic stability will be achieved through the mark of the beast. If you have a debit card, you know how easy it is to pay for something or to take money out of your checking account. Whereas you borrow money with a credit card, you simply gain access to your own money with a debit card. It is so easy.

Why do we need a card? Why couldn't we just have a mark in our hand or forehead that could be scanned? Thirty years ago, we had no idea how the mark of the beast would work. Today it would be a piece of cake, and it will appeal to the vast majority of people who make a living by working. The rebellion against welfare fraud will demand a stable economic system. The Antichrist will promise world peace and economic stability, and he will accomplish both for awhile. The world will flock to him and worship him.

He is attractive, appealing. He is given the crown of victory, but not sovereignty. He conquers in his own name by common consent. A typical politician, he promises what he cannot deliver for the long term — unity, stability, and peace. The red horse rider destroys the myth of the white horse rider.

The red horse rider: War (6:3-4)

And when he had opened the second seal, I heard the second beast say, Come and see. And there went out another horse that was red: and power was given to him that sat thereon to take peace from the earth, and that they should kill one another: and there was given unto him a great sword (6:3-4).

This rider takes peace from the earth. Military warfare breaks out in a real world war or series of wars which continue till the Second Coming of the Lord Jesus Christ.

No man or organization can guarantee peace while the red horse rider has power.

Students of warfare already know the identity of the next rider.

The black horse rider: Famine (6:5-6)

And when he had opened the third seal, I heard the third beast say, Come and see. And I beheld, and lo a black horse; and he that sat on him had a pair of balances in his hand. And I heard a voice in the midst of the four beasts say, A measure of wheat for a penny, and three measures of barley for a penny; and see thou hurt not the oil and the wine (6:5-6).

Worldwide famine will follow war. Famine always follows war because of the devastated landscape.

A denarius (KJV "penny") was a day's wage. A working man will not be able to support his family, having to spend a day's wages for a loaf of bread.

The rich will still enjoy oil and wine, symbols of luxury, but not the poor, who will have only the barest necessities. Many of the poor will no doubt starve to death because of Famine, who rides the black horse.

Famine is awful, but the next rider is almost beyond belief.

The pale horse rider: Death (6:7-8)

And when he had opened the fourth seal, I heard the voice of the fourth beast say, Come and see. And I looked, and behold a pale horse: and his name that sat on him was Death, and Hell followed with him. And power was given unto them over the fourth part of the earth, to kill with sword, and with hunger, and with death, and with the beasts of the earth (6:7-8)

"Behold" indicates John was startled by what he saw. The horse is an unearthly color, literally pale green, and its rider is Death. The appearance of this horse and its rider blows John's mind.

Death is given power to kill one-fourth of the earth's population. The earth's population is currently estimated at some six billion people. The United States has less than half a billion people. Over three times the population of the United States, approximately 1,500,000,000 people, will be killed by Death, the pale horse rider.

This other-worldly rider kills with sword (military power), famine, death (pestilence), and (wild) beasts. He has awesome and indefensible power.

Hell (*hades*) follows. Death kills physically, and Hell claims the souls spiritually. Hell is happy to ride along with Death and to claim souls for eternal damnation and separation from God.

Death rides unbridled during the Great Tribulation and is destroyed at the Great White Throne judgment. Jesus himself indicated that if the Great Tribulation time were not shortened everybody on earth would die:

> *And except those days be shortened, there should no flesh be saved: but for the elect's sake those days shall be shortened (Matt 24:22).*

The end of Death and Hell will come only after the second coming of Christ and his millennial reign upon earth. This will be the final evidence of Christ's triumph over Satan's diabolical scheme against mankind:

> *And death and hell were cast into the lake of fire. This is the second death (Rev 20:14).*

Jesus gave the pattern for the Great Tribulation Period. In Matthew 24:5-8, note the deceit (white horse rider), wars (red horse rider), famines (black horse rider), and pestilences (pale horse rider):

> *For many shall come in my name, saying, I am Christ; and shall deceive many. And ye shall hear of wars and rumours of wars: see that ye be not troubled: for all these things ust come to pass, but the end is not yet. For nation shall rise against nation, and kingdom against kingdom: and there shall be famines, and pestilences, and earthquakes, in divers places. All these are the beginning of sorrows.*

The Day of God's Divine Wrath (6:9-17)

This may just shock you! If your idea of Heaven is one of sitting down and having a little talk with Jesus and of kicking back in a rocking chair while Grandfather God tells you a bedtime story or listens to you tell about your life on earth, you will be surprised. If you think nothing other than peaceful thoughts will ever enter the minds of those on the heavenly shore, think again. A plaintive cry goes up for vengeance and the execution of righteousness. It's a cry that will be answered later, and woe be unto those who experience the wrath of the Lion, Jesus Christ.

The cry for vengeance (6:9-11)

> *And when he had opened the fifth seal, I saw under the altar the souls of them that were slain for the word of God, and for the testimony which they*

held: and they cried with a loud voice, saying, How long, O Lord, holy and true, dost thou not judge and avenge our blood on them that dwell on the earth? And white robes were given unto every one of them; and it was said unto them, that they should rest yet for a little season, until their fellowservants also and their brethren, that should be killed as they were, should be fulfilled (6:9-11).

The scene shifts to Heaven, and John sees those who will be martyred for their faith in Christ. This probably includes both Old Testament and Tribulation saints. I do not believe Old Testament saints will be resurrected when the church is raptured, because the church is a distinct and unique body of believers from the Day of Pentecost to the Rapture. We are the bride of Christ, and the Old Testament saints must wait just a little while longer. They, along with the Tribulation martyrs, will be resurrected in conjunction with the second coming.

They are seen under the altar where Jesus offered his blood for the sins of the world, whether symbolically or literally. Many people believe that Jesus literally went to Heaven and presented his blood to God the Father as a sacrifice for our sins after his death. As evidence of that, they cite Hebrews 9:23-24.

It was therefore necessary that the patterns of things in the heavens should be purified with these; but the heavenly things themselves with better sacrifices than these. For Christ is not entered into the holy places made with hands, which are the figures of the true; but into heaven itself, now to apear in the presence of God for us: . . .

Whether Jesus went symbolically or literally, these under the altar cry for vengeance, but are told to wait a little longer because more must yet die. It may be that a majority of those who trust Christ in the Great Tribulation will be put to death. I believe that most who trust Jesus during the Tribulation will die martyrs' deaths.

They are given white robes of righteousness, which brings to mind an interesting question: If their bodies are in the ground, and their souls are in Heaven – John can see their souls – then what kind of bodies do they have? They do not yet have their resurrected and glorified bodies, so they must have temporary bodies. It is not a body of earth, as we now have, and it is not a resurrection body of flesh and bones which we are given at Christ's return. I do not pretend to have the answer to this question. Just think how many books I could sell if I did!

The cry of the martyrs for vengeance is answered, "Wait a while longer."

The day of divine wrath (6:12-17)

The breaking of the sixth seal ushers in the last half of the Great Tribulation. The first five seals will be opened in the first three and one-half years. We have just covered three and one-half years. It will take us a long time to cover those last three and one-half years as we see what the Lord Jesus Christ is going to do.

Great convulsions will shake the earth, and geography will be drastically altered.

And I beheld when he had opened the sixth seal, and lo, there was a great earthquake; and the sun became black as sackcloth of hair, and the moon became as blood; and the stars of heaven fell unto the earth, even as a fig tree casteth her untimely figs, when she is shaken of a mighty wind.   And the heaven departed as a scroll when it is rolled together; and every mountain and island were moved out of their places (6:12-14).

The Lord Jesus Christ takes the universe and gives it a good shaking. He created the universe, and he is going to shake it violently. There will be a recognition, a dawning, that the Antichrist is not really in charge after all. There is a higher power. Every mountain and island are moved.

All levels of society are affected and seek to escape the wrath of the Lamb through death. Those who succeed in dying must still face Christ at the Great White Throne. No one escapes.

And the kings of the earth, and the great men, and the rich men, and the chief captains, and the mighty men, and every bondman, and every free man, hid themselves in the dens and in the rocks of the mountains; and said to the mountains and rocks, Fall on us, and hide us from the face of him that sitteth on the throne, and from the wrath of the Lamb: for the great day of his wrath is come; and who shall be able to stand? (6:15-17)

Where will you stand?

"Who shall be able to stand?" The answer is obvious: only those who accept God's grace, though they may die the death of the martyr.

God is righteous. God is holy. God hates that which is contrary to himself. Jehovah is a Man of War, strong and mighty, mighty in battle. Though the modern mind is reluctant to believe that God will judge the wicked, the Bible teaches that he will. God will judge you severely if you do not accept his Son. There is a day coming when the wrath of the Lamb will be revealed. Jesus is the Lamb of God, but he is not a toy. He is the Lion of the tribe of Judah, and he will bring judgment to this earth and to those who reject him. He is Lord, not a lackey! He will never die again, because he is the King of kings and Lord of lords. His wrath will be revealed.

But I have good news! You do not have to go through the Great Tribulation. You do not have to face Jesus as an angry Judge at the Great White Throne. You can be in Heaven when all hell breaks loose on earth. You can accept Jesus Christ as your personal Lord and Savior right now and experience eternal life, or you can reject him and experience eternal death. The choice is yours, because God loves you too much to force you to be saved.

Where will you spend eternity? If you reject Jesus, you will spend it first in Hell and then in the lake of fire, separated from God and from all that is good for all eternity. If you accept him as your Savior, your Sacrifice, your Substitute, you will experience eternal life in the very presence of God. The choice is yours. Where will you stand?

2

TRIBULATION SAINTS

Revelation 7:1-17

That wasn't so bad, was it?

Oh sure, there's the problem of where Mt. Everest went, but most people probably weren't planning to visit there during the Great Tribulation anyway. And surely Great Britain, Australia, Hawaii, and Cuba will be located in a matter of days by spy satellites.

One-fourth of all mankind have an appointment with the pale horse rider, Death, but, hey, the odds are three to one against dying so far.

Frankly, things have been quite peaceful. The white horse rider, Antichrist, has established a treaty with Israel, guaranteeing her peace for seven years. But the opening of the sixth seal in chapter six signals the beginning of the last three and one-half years, and peace becomes a mere illusion. Hell on earth is the order of the day.

Let's put on our thinking caps for a moment.

Will it be possible for people who have heard the gospel during the church age to be saved during the Great Tribulation? I don't know. It's a risky game to play. Will it be possible for anybody to turn to Christ and be saved during the Great Tribulation? In 2 Thessalonians 2:7, the Bible clearly teaches that the Holy Spirit, who restrains evil in this age, will be taken out of the world when the church is raptured. Since the Holy Spirit is the agent of salvation, how can anybody get saved when he is gone?

The Scriptures indicate that a great multitude of Jews and Gentiles will trust in the Lord after the church is caught up to be with the Lord in glory. You may be surprised to find that during the Devil's holiday, when the Holy Spirit no longer restrains evil on the earth, men and women by the millions will come to Christ.

The Vision of Five Angels (7:1-3)

And after these things I saw four angels standing on the four corners of the earth, holding the four winds of the earth, that the wind should not blow on the earth, nor on the sea, nor on any tree. And I saw another angel ascending from the east, having the seal of the living God: and he cried with a loud voice to the four angels, to whom it was given to hurt the earth and the sea, saying, Hurt not the earth, neither the sea, nor the trees, till we have sealed the servants of our God in their foreheads (7:1-3).

The work of the Holy Spirit

To set this in a proper context, let's first look at the work of the Holy Spirit. The purpose of the Holy Spirit in this age is to call out the church and present it to Christ as his bride. The Rapture ends that ministry. The church is unique as the body of Christ and will be unique throughout eternity as the bride of Christ. The Holy Spirit also restrains evil so the gospel can spread throughout the earth during this age. I hate to think what the earth would be like without the restraint of the Holy Spirit.

The Holy Spirit has always been present, because he is omnipresent. People were saved before Pentecost, when his abode was in Heaven. When Christ went back to Heaven, he said he would send a Comforter (*paraclete*) to go beside us, and he identified that one as the Holy Spirit. The Spirit has made earth his home base since that time.

Christ was here in the Old Testament as the Angel of Jehovah, but he didn't live here. The Spirit will work in a different way than now. His abode will no longer be here after the Rapture, but he will be present and active. More will be saved during the Great Tribulation than in any other seven-year period in history. They are called saints, not the church. The church will already be in Heaven when these Tribulation saints turn to Christ.

Now let's turn our attention to the first of several interludes in the Book of Revelation.

The purpose of the interlude (7:1-3)

Between the sixth and seventh seals, there is an interlude as four angels hold back the winds of judgment while God sets apart and protects his servants. A fifth angel gives the orders.

He cries with a "loud voice" (*phone megale*), from which we get megaphone. Every cheerleader and everyone who has ever been to a football game knows that a megaphone amplifies the voice. The fifth angel speaks with a thunderous voice, which in the military would be called a command voice.

God's servants are to be sealed with a mark in their foreheads; otherwise, they would not survive the judgments to come.

The Sealing of the Twelve Tribes (7:4-8)

And I heard the number of them which were sealed: and there were sealed an hundred and forty and four thousand of all the tribes of the children of Israel.   Of the tribe of Juda were sealed twelve thousand.   Of the tribe of Reuben were sealed twelve thousand.   Of the tribe of Gad were sealed twelve thousand.   Of the tribe of Aser were sealed twelve thousand.   Of the tribe of Nepthalim were sealed twelve thousand.   Of the tribe of Manasses were sealed twelve thousand. Of the tribe of Simeon were sealed twelve thousand.   Of the tribe of Levi were sealed twelve thousand. Of the tribe of Issacher were sealed twelve thousand. Of the tribe of Zabulon were sealed twelve thousand. Of the tribe of Joseph were sealed twelve thousand.   Of the tribe of Benjamin were sealed twelve thousand (7:4-8).

The detail is amazing and about as boring to read as some of the "begat" or genealogical passages in the Bible. But the detail is necessary.

Many have claimed to be the 144,000. Only one group can ever rightly claim this identification, and they don't even know it. The other claimants are wrong.

Who they are (7:4-8)

The 144,000 can easily be identified — they are the twelve tribes of Israel, 12,000 per tribe.

Jews today do not know their tribes, but God has no question in his mind. None of the tribes are lost as far as God is concerned.

These 144,000 are the ones who will witness of Christ in the Great Tribulation. Jesus himself said so:

And this gospel of the kingdom shall be preached in all the world for a witness unto all nations, and then shall the end come (Matt 24:14).

Other Israelites will be saved, but many will die martyrs' deaths. These 144,000 will be brought safely through. They are sealed and protected.

If you know your Bible history, you recognize that there is a difference in the tribes blessed by Jacob and those presented here. Ephraim and Dan are omitted.

Ephraim and Manasses were the sons of Joseph. Joseph did not receive a portion, but both of his sons did in the Old Testament. Levi did not receive a portion, because the Levites were to be the tribe of priests supported by all the other tribes.

Ephraim led in the division of the kingdom. Dan led in apostasy and may be the source of the Antichrist because of the apostate nature of that tribe. Joseph replaces Ephraim, and Levi replaces Dan for world evangelism.

Who they are not

There is no need to spiritualize. "Israel" means Israel, descendants of Jacob.

False teaching abounds on this subject. Everybody wants to be Israel. Everybody wants to have the blessings promised to Israel in the Abrahamic and Davidic Covenants. But everybody cannot be Israel.

Israel is not the church nor any other group in existence today. It is not the United States. It is not the Jehovah's Witnesses, nor any lost tribe of Mormons residing in the Arctic Circle and planning to come south to Independence, Missouri, to establish the New Jerusalem.

Again, there is no need to spiritualize — God will seal 144,000 Israelites to evangelize the world. They will do in seven years what the church has not done in 2,000 years, i.e., reach the whole world with the gospel of Jesus Christ.

The Martyred Dead of the Great Tribulation (7:9-17)

The interlude also includes a peek at the Gentiles who will be saved and martyred during the Great Tribulation.

They are Gentiles (7:9-12)

After this I beheld, and lo, a great multitude, which no man could number, of all nations, and kindreds, and people, and tongues, stood before the throne, and before the Lamb, clothed with white robes, and palms in their hands. And cried with a loud voice, saying, Salvation to our God which sitteth upon the throne, and unto the Lamb.

And all the angels stood round about the throne, and about the elders, and the four beasts, and fell before the throne on their faces, and worshipped God, saying, Amen: Blessing, and glory, and wisdom, and thanksgiving, and honour, and power, and might, be unto our God for ever and ever. Amen (7:9-12).

Millions of Gentiles from all nations, kindreds, peoples, and tongues will come to Christ. Most will be martyred, but they will wear white robes of righteousness and have palms of victory in Jesus in their hands. It's the righteousness of Christ and his victory over death that spell victory for saints of all ages.

It's not just our little group that's going to be in Heaven, but a stupendous multitude. Surprise, surprise! Some of us will need an attitude adjustment when we encounter Heaven's diverse throng of redeemed sinners.

The angels join in a sevenfold ascription of praise to God for his attributes and goodness, but not for salvation because they are sinless creatures, not redeemed sinners (7:11-12). The song of redemption is one holy angels cannot sing. God offered the angels who followed Lucifer in his rebellion no second chance. What a wonderful Savior we serve, who gave his own life to reconcile lost mankind to God! What a wonderful privilege we have to be the children of God, brothers and sisters of Christ, redeemed by the blood of the Lamb!

They are Great Tribulation martyrs (7:13-17)

And one of the elders answered, saying unto me, What are these which are arrayed in white robes? and whence came they?

And I said unto him, Sir, thou knowest.

And he said to me, These are they which came out of great tribulation, and have washed their robes, and made them white in the blood of the Lamb. Therefore are they before the throne of God, and serve him day and night in his temple: and he that sitteth on the throne shall dwell among them. They shall hunger no more, neither thirst any more; neither shall the sun light on them, nor any heat. For the Lamb which is in the midst of the throne shall feed them, and shall lead them unto living fountains of waters: and God shall wipe away all tears from their eyes (7:13-17).

If the elders represent the church, and they do, this group is a different body of saints. This is extremely important.

An elder asks John who they are. John's answer is, "Sir, you know I don't know. You tell me who they are." If they had been the church, John would have known. John is a part of the church. They are not the church! The church will not go through the Great Tribulation.

Jesus has other sheep not of the church and not of Israel. His sheep include the Great Tribulation saints and the Millennium saints. It no doubt shocked Israel to hear Jesus say,

> *And other sheep I have, which are not of this fold: them also I must bring, and they shall hear my voice; and there shall be one fold, and one shepherd (John 10:16)*

Upon John's admission that he does not know who the multitude are, the elder replies that they are Great Tribulation saints, martyrs who have sealed their testimony with their own blood. Some will die of earthquakes, war, famine, or pestilence from the pale horse rider. Many will be hounded to death by the world ruler, much as the Jews were in World War II. The anti-Semitic movement of the Great Tribulation will make the holocaust of World War II pale in comparison. And the anti-Christ movement will be unparalleled in the history of mankind. Antichrist, the man, will not only be an imitator of Christ, but will also be the arch enemy of Christ. He will outlaw anything having to do with Christ and will systematically hunt down and kill anyone who trusts Christ. That is why the seal of the 144,000 Jewish evangelists is so important.

The marytrs have trwashed their robes and made them white in the blood of the Lamb, the only way to do it. His blood is the only cleansing agent for sin. His blood was the only thing that made you clean.

Delivered from their afflictions, these will serve the Lord for eternity. The tears of their suffering will be wiped away by the Savior who died for them and for whom they gave their lives.

I saw a sign recently that posed this question: "Jesus died for you – what are you willing to do for him?" The Great Tribulation martyrs will not recant their testimonies, will not accept the mark of the beast, but will die for their faith. I wonder how many of us would do the same thing.

It's the Blood

God is going to judge Israel and the world, but 12,000 from each tribe of Israel, totalling 144,000, will be sealed and protected from the judgments. A great multitude of Gentiles will be saved during the Great Tribulation, but many, if not most, will be martyred. Even in the tragic closing days that precede the Second Coming of Christ to the earth, countless souls will trust him as Savior and be saved by his grace. And every one of them will be saved, not by their own deaths, but by the sacrificial death of Jesus Christ on Calvary.

Although it may offend you and may not be suited to the so-called sophistication of the twentieth century, the blood of Christ is exceedingly precious in the sight of God the Father and is the only cleansing agent for sin. If you miss Hell, it will be by the blood. If you reach Heaven, it will be by the blood. "What can wash away my sin? What can make me whole again? Nothing but the blood of Jesus. For my pardon this I see; for my cleansing, this my plea — nothing but the blood of Jesus. Nothing can for sin atone; naught of good that I have done — nothing but the blood of Jesus."

Millions will come to Christ and be saved, but that's not your problem, is it? Your problem is your own salvation. Are you saved? Are you washed in the blood of the Lamb?

3

FIRST FOUR TRUMPETS

Revelation 8:1-13

Only the seventh seal remains to be opened after the parenthesis of Chapter 7. This is John's pattern in the Book of Revelation. He gives the first six of whatever the series is, then presents parenthetical material to help us understand. Finally, he opens the seventh of the series, which introduces the next series of seven. Got it?

The seven seals represent judgment resulting from man's willful activity.

The seven trumpets announce judgment as a direct activity of God.

The seven personalities reveal judgment resulting from Satan's fight against God.

And the seven bowls of wrath contain the final judgment of the Great Tribulation.

When symbols are used, their meaning is supplied. There is no need for fanaticism or sensationalism. God says what he means! Judgment is coming to the earth.

Praise the Lord! Jesus will make everything right. Count on it.

God does not change. The God of the Old Testament who brought judgment upon the unrighteous earth has not changed. He's the God of the New Testament, and his nature is still unalterably opposed to wickedness. He would not be God if he did not judge unrighteousness.

The Seventh Seal (8:1)

> *And when he had opened the seventh seal, there was silence in heaven about the space of half an hour (8:1).*

Opening the last seal

The Lord Jesus Christ is in full command. He alone can and does break the seventh seal of the book that Daniel sealed, title deed to earth.

He now acts as Judge. He died as a Lamb, even for those who reject him. Men are lost because they reject Christ. If not your Savior, then Jesus will be your Judge. He brings judgment upon the wicked earth.

The righteous have always wondered why the wicked seemed to prosper and why God did not judge the wicked. The martyrs around the throne (Rev 6:10) asked the same question. The millennia of questions will be answered in the Great Tribulation. God does not march to our timetable – and I'm so glad – but at the proper time he will make all things right.

Contained in the seventh seal are all the subsequent developments leading to the Second Coming of Christ, including the trumpets and bowls. All of the the awful plagues and judgments are freed and authorized when the seventh seal is broken.

Silence in Heaven

What a solemn scene! There is a heavenly hush, total silence in Heaven for half an hour. It is a lull, the calm before the storm.

Silence is a strange phenomenon in Heaven. If there were time in Heaven, praises would ring out to the Lord 24 hours a day, seven days a week, 52 weeks a year, forever. Suddenly, there's a hush, a deadly silence. The moment is pregnant with anticipation, the situation too serious for words. Total, uninterrupted silence.

It's a silence like that of a courtroom just before the jury foreman reads a verdict. Do you remember the anticipation just before the O.J. Simpson verdict was read? Everything was hushed. Imagine that scene in Heaven where the verdict is about to be read. Silence.

Why is there such a strange silence? When the sixth seal was broken and nature responded with a mighty convulsion, brave men might have weakened (Rev 6:12-17). God, in his patience, gives them time to repent.

God patiently waits, even as he does now.

This silence marks the transition from grace to judgment. It indicates something momentous is about to take place. Earth's sentence is about to be read.

The Seven Angels (8:2-6)

And I saw the seven angels which stood before God; and to them were given seven trumpets.

And another angel came and stood at the altar, having a golden censer; and there was given unto him much incense, that he should offer it with the prayers of all saints upon the golden altar which was before the throne. And the smoke of the incense, which came with the prayers of the saints, ascended up before God out of the angel's hand. And the angel took the censer, and filled it with fire of the altar, and cast it into the earth: and there were voices, and thunderings, and lightnings, and an earthquake. And the seven angels which had the seven trumpets prepared themselves to sound (8:2-6).

Their trumpets (8:2)

In the wilderness wanderings of Israel, it took seven trumpets to move Israel. These seven trumpets will have the effect of moving Israel into Palestine. Israel will be regathered into Palestine, eventually to claim all the territory given to her by God in the Abrahamic Covenant.

Trumpets were an important part of every major event in Israel. As the trumpets of Israel were used at Jericho, and as the walls of opposition came tumbling down, so these tribulation trumpets signal that world opposition to God is about to crumble.

There is no relation here to the "last trump." That trumpet is the voice of the glorified Christ at the Rapture. These are judgment trumpets.

Their purpose (8:3-6)

Many think the angel in 8:3 is Christ. Not so, as he is no longer Intercessor for the church, because the church has already been delivered and is in Heaven. Christ does not need to go to the altar again. He has already made his sacrifice upon the altar. He sacrificed himself.

As burning incense filled the Tabernacle, so the prayers of saints fill Heaven and ascend to God. The prayers of the martyrs for vengeance (6:9-11) will now be answered because of Christ's name and sacrifice.

The Old Testament high priest took fire off the altar and carried it into the Holy of holies. Here it is reversed: the censer is taken out of Heaven and hurled to the earth in answer to prayer. The earth shudders or quakes in response.

The angels prepare to shatter the silence by blowing the trumpets of literal plagues. These are as literal as the plagues on Egypt. I'm constantly amazed by those who try to make the entire Book of Revelation symbolic. They will readily accept that the plagues on Egypt during Moses' time were literal, but will absolutely reject any idea that a loving God would bring literal plagues upon the earth again. They will even admit he is the same unchanging God in one breath and deny literal judgment in the next.

Yes, he can, and yes, he will.

The Four Trumpets (8:7-13)

The first four trumpets are the easy ones; the last three are awful. The last three are called the "woe" trumpets.

First trumpet: plague on the land (8:7)

The first angel sounded, and there followed hail and fire mingled with blood, and they were cast upon the earth: and the third part of trees was burnt up, and all green grass was burnt up (8:7).

Can you imagine what the earth will look like after the first trumpet? God first used the Flood, now fire for global judgment and purification of the earth.

Hail, fire, and blood destroy one-third of all plant life. Plant life was first created, and it is first destroyed. The plague upon plant life in Egypt was literal. So is this.

> *So there was hail, and fire mingled with the hail, very grievous, such as there was none like it in all the land of Egypt since it became a nation. And the hail smote throughout all the land of Egypt all that was in the field, both man and beast; and the hail smote every herb of the field, and brake every tree of the field. Only in the land of Goshen, where the children of Israel were, was there no hail (Exod 9:24-26).*

Same unchanging and holy God. He promised not to destroy the earth by water again. He won't. He likewise promised to destroy the earth by fire. He will.

The first trumpet is a plague upon plant life on the land. The second is a plague upon the sea.

Second trumpet: plague on the sea (8:8-9)

> *And the second angel sounded, and as it were a great mountain burning with fire was cast into the sea: and the third part of the sea became blood: and the third part of the creatures which were in the sea, and had life, died; and the third part of the ships were destroyed (8:8-9).*

A literal and tangible mass resembling ("as it were") a great mountain afire is cast into the literal sea. One-third becomes literal blood, and one-third of the literal creatures in the literal sea die a literal death. Also, one-third of the literal ships (and literal sailors) are literally destroyed.

The sea occupies most of the earth's surface, and it is subject to the direct judgment of God. Vacations to the beach will be over. Dead fish and bodies of men will wash up all over the world, as will the wreckage from ships.

Third trumpet: plague on fresh water (8:10-11)

And the third angel sounded, and there fell a great star from heaven, burning as it were a lamp, and it fell upon the third part of the rivers, and upon the fountains of waters: and the name of the star is called Wormwood: and the third part of the waters became wormwood; and many men died of the waters, because they were made bitter (8:10-11).

A literal meteor contaminates one-third of the earth's fresh water, and many men die. I wondered how it was possible for one meteor to contaminate a third of the fresh water of the earth. The thought came to me, "What if a meteor hit one of the great lakes in the northern part of the United States?" Think how many downstream rivers would be affected. The effect would be enormous. The possibility is not far-fetched at all.

It is so important to know your Old Testament before trying to understand the Revelation, because the two are so intertwined. The tree made the bitter waters sweet at Marah (Exodus 15:23-25), but here the wormwood cast into the sweet water makes it bitter.

Moses' tree pointed to the cross. On the cross, Christ the Savior made believing men's eternity sweet. "Wormwood" suggests judgment for idolatry and injustice.

The Savior becomes the Judge. The Lamb of God becomes the Lion of the tribe of Judah.

Fourth trumpet: plague on the heavens (8:12-13)

Food has been destroyed, shipping crippled, and water supply limited. Now God puts out one-third of the earth's light, which must radically alter the laws of nature.

> *And the fourth angel sounded, and the third part of the sun was smitten, and the third part of the moon, and the third part of the stars; so as the third part of them was darkened, and the day shone not for a third part of it, and the night likewise (8:12).*

This is not a problem for the Creator. Can you imagine not having a third of the natural light we have now? I expect a big chill from the loss of sunshine. The crime rate will no doubt soar with the additional hours of darkness.

The beauty of earth's vegetation and the seas, the blessings of fresh water, the light and life of the sun, moon, and stars, are all dramatically plagued by the Lord Jesus Christ. Mankind will have to recognize the power and sovereignty of Almighty God. The Antichrist cannot hold a candle to the power of the Lord Jesus Christ.

As terrible as these plagues are, they pale in comparison with those to come, the "woe" trumpets announced by an angel or "eagle."

> *And I beheld, and heard an angel flying through the midst of heaven, saying with a loud voice, Woe, woe, woe, to the inhabitants of the earth by reason of the other voices of the trumpet of the three angels, which are yet to sound (8:13).*

It gets even worse. You don't want to be here for the Great Tribulation.

Are you still playing games with God?

It may be difficult for you in this day of grace to picture your Lord Jesus Christ directing the catastrophic judgments which the Bible clearly indicates will come upon this earth. But the Word of God is plain, and men are called to avail themselves of the grace of God before it is too late. Today is the day of salvation.

We cannot keep this judgment from coming to the earth, but we can get the Word of God out and reduce the population that will be left on the earth so that fewer people will have to go through the Great Tribulation. Let's take all we can with us to Heaven when we go.

How about you? Do you still think God is playing games? A casual reading of the Book of Revelation will tell you different. Do you still think you can outsmart him? Satan, who is much smarter than you, has been trying to outsmart God for untold thousands of years without success. Do you still reject his grace? If so, you'd better be prepared for hell on earth, because these plagues are for you.

Won't you trust Christ now in this silent calm before the storm? God has given you this time to repent. Don't miss it.

4

TRUMPETS FIVE AND SIX

Revelation 9:1-21

The breaking of the seventh seal introduced the seven trumpets. Four trumpets have sounded. The first brought the plague upon plant life, the second the plague upon the sea, the third the plague upon fresh water, and the fourth the plague upon the sun, moon, and stars. They were awful to contemplate, their results disastrous and deadly. But while the judgments of the first four trumpets were bad, they were nothing compared to the plagues to come. The first four trumpets merely serve as attention-getters.

The next three trumpets are "woe" trumpets, according to Revelation 8:13 —

> *And I beheld, and heard an angel flying through the midst of heaven, saying with a loud voice, Woe, woe, woe, to the inhabiters of the earth by reason of the other voices of the trumpet of the three angels, which are yet to sound!*

The church is in Heaven, and the Holy Spirit restrains evil no longer.   Trumpets five and six introduce unrestrained demonic torment upon a Christ-rejecting world. The Lamb is the Judge, but he judges as a Lion.

Fifth Trumpet: First Woe (9:1-12)

We now are allowed a brief glimpse of the demonic empire led by Satan himself. Sometimes we get so wrapped up worrying about people that make our lives miserable, our circumstances, our order of worship, and our doctrine, that we forget Paul's admonition to know who our enemy really is. Satan must delight in keeping our attention diverted from the real threat.

> *Put on the whole armour of God, that ye may be able to stand against the wiles of the devil. For we wrestle not against flesh and blood, but against principalities, against powers, against the rulers of the darkness of this world, against spiritual wickedness in high places (Eph 6:11-12).*

Demonic warfare is real, and the Revelation that unveils the glorified Christ also unmasks the diabolic horde.

The fallen star (9:1-2)

> *And the fifth angel sounded, and I saw a star fall from heaven unto the earth: and to him was given the key of the bottomless pit. And he opened the bottomless pit; and there arose a smoke out of the pit, as the smoke of a great furnace; and the sun and the air were darkened by reason of the smoke of the pit (9:1-2).*

The star is a person ("him") who acts with intelligence, and who receives and uses the key to the bottomless pit, or abyss. I think we know who the star is.

The star is no doubt Satan himself, but he is a fallen star, "son of the morning":

> *How art thou fallen from heaven, O Lucifer, son of the morning! how art thou cut down to the ground, which didst weaken the nations! (Isa 14:12).*

Jesus said,

> *I beheld Satan as lightning fall from heaven (Luke 10:18).*

John "saw a star fall from heaven unto the earth" (Rev 9:1).

The abyss (bottomless pit) is the abode of demons. While talking to the demoniac of Gadara, Jesus gave us some insight on this place.

> *And Jesus asked him, saying, What is thy name? And he said, Legion: because many devils were entered into him. And they besought him that he would not command them to go out into the deep (Luke 8:30-31).*

The "deep" is the bottomless pit or abyss and the place Satan will be confined a thousand years during the millennial kingdom immediately after the Great Tribulation and the Battle of Armageddon.

> *And I saw an angel come down from heaven, having the key of the bottomless pit and a great chain in his hand. And he laid hold on the dragon, that old serpent, which is the Devil, and Satan, and bound*

> *him a thousand years, and cast him into the bottomless pit, and shut him up, and set a seal upon him, that he should deceive the nations no more, till the thousand years should be fulfilled: and after that he must be loosed a little season (Rev 20:1-3).*

The abyss may be synonymous with Hell (*hades*):

> *For if God spared not the angels that sinned, but cast them down to hell, and delivered them into chains of darkness, to be reserved unto judgment . . .(2 Pet 2:4).*

Many of the angels that followed Lucifer in his rebellion against God are apparently bound in Hell. Can you imagine what would happen if they were all loosed upon the earth? Though I cannot say it with certainty, I believe the fallen angels are the demons who serve Satan today.

Christ now has the key to the abyss, having defeated death, hell, and the grave in his resurrection. He will give the key to Satan. When Satan opens the pit (9:2), that which is contained therein erupts like a volcano, polluting the air and darkening the sky. Physical and spiritual (demonic) oppression follows upon the earth. Demons will run wild, unrestricted and unrestrained.

The plague of demonic locusts (9:3-6)

> *And there came out of the smoke locusts upon the earth: and unto them was given power, as the scorpions of the earth have power. And it was commanded them that they should not hurt the grass of the earth, neither any green thing, neither any tree; but only those men which have not the seal of God in their foreheads. And to them it was given that they*

should not kill them, but that they should be tormented five months: and their torment was as the torment of a scorpion, when he striketh a man. And in those days shall men seek death, and shall not find it; and shall desire to die, and death shall flee from them (9:3-6).

These are literal locusts, but unusual:
1. They eat no vegetation. Normally, locusts thrive on green plants.
2. They have a king, probably a demon warlord whose name means "destruction" or "destroyer."

These are uncanny denizens of the deep, locusts of a hellish species, animated by demonic instincts, and equipped with infernal powers. They torment Christ-rejecting people for five months with the sting like that of a scorpion, which is extremely painful and which can make a person deathly ill.

The demonic affliction is so great that men will not even be able to exercise their will to commit suicide. Only those sealed by God will escape the torment of these locusts.

The description of demonic locusts (9:7-12)

And the shapes of the locusts were like unto horses prepared unto battle; and on their heads were as it were crowns like gold, and their faces were as the faces of men. And they had hair as the hair of women, and their teeth were as the teeth of lions. And they had breastplates, as it were breastplates of iron; and the sound of their wings was as the sound of chariots of many horses running to battle. And they had tails like unto scorpions, and there were stings in their tails: and their power was to hurt men five months. And they had a king over them, which is the angel of the bottomless pit, whose name in the Hebrew tongue is Abaddon, but in the Greek tongue hath his name Apollyon.

One woe is past; and, behold, there come two woes more hereafter (9:7-12).

You may think this is some fanciful writing of a man who has heartburn after a late-night supper of Mexican food, but it isn't. There is a demonic world that is real, if largely unseen. God has protected us from seeing everything that is going on around us.

LSD-guru Timothy Leary said if we could see what he saw while tripping on acid it would scare us to death. His description of demons was uncanny in its similarity to the biblical account. I believe in his altered state of mind on drugs he was permitted to see some of the very demons of Hell. Demons are real.

Revelation unveils Jesus Christ and also exposes the true nature of Satan and his emissaries as well as the wickedness of man. When Christ is revealed, the opposition is likewise revealed in all its ugliness in contrast to the righteousness and holiness of Christ.

These intruments of divine justice are frightful, indestructible, fast, unavoidable, utterly evil, unfeeling, and ugly (shaped as horses with men's faces, women's hair, lions' teeth, scorpions' tails, breastplates, wings, and crowns). Their appearance is hideous!

Their wings make a sound as of many horses and chariots running to battle (attack helicopters, perhaps?). The nearest I can come to the clop-clop-clop of many horses is the wop-wop-wop of hundreds or thousands of helicopter rotor blades. Since we don't have many horses pulling chariots today, we'll have to go with something to which we can relate, and the sound of helicopters is something we have all heard.

Under the inspiration of the Holy Spirit, John relates what he sees to things that are familiar. The terms "as" and "as it were" tip us off that John may be using symbolic language. Otherwise, he could never describe the demonic horde of locusts in ways we could comprehend.

This first woe covers five months of the last three and one-half years of the Great Tribulation, and it gets worse. Calamity continues.

Sixth Trumpet: Second Woe (9:13-21)

For five months, Christ-rejecting men have wanted to commit suicide, but could not. The oppression of the demonic locusts will be soon forgotten under the plague of the sixth trumpet.

Loosing of four angels (9:13-15)

And the sixth angel sounded, and I heard a voice from the four horns of the altar which is before God, saying to the sixth angel which had the trumpet, Loose the four angels which are bound in the great river Euphrates. And the four angels were loosed, which were prepared for an hour, and a day, and a month, and a year, for to slay the third part of men (9:13-15).

The golden altar is the place of prayer. The prayers of the martyrs are being answered (Revelation 6:10).

Four evil and prepared angels are bound in the Euphrates River. The Euphrates River area is Mesopotamia, or the Cradle of Civilization in history. It was the site of the Garden of Eden, first sin of man, first murder, first war, beginning of the Flood, Tower of Babel, Babylonian captivity of Israel, idolatry's home. It is in modern-day Iraq, and has always been identified with man's rebellion against God.

The Euphrates location indicates an invasion from the Orient. Napoleon said, "China is a sleeping giant, and God pity the generation that wakes her up." The Tribulation generation will apparently have that distinction. The white man's day is just about over.

The four angels are prepared to execute God's timetable to the appointed hour. They exist to kill one-third (another 1.5 billion or so) of mankind. Wholesale slaughter comes after the five months of the fifth trumpet when men cannot die.

The army of 200 million (9:16-19)

And the number of the army of the horsemen were two hundred thousand thousand: and I heard the number of them.

And thus I saw the horses in the vision, and them that sat on them, having breastplates of fire, and of jacinth, and brimstone: and the heads of the horses were as the heads of lions; and out of their mouths issued fire and smoke and brimstone. By these three was the third part of men killed, by the fire, and by the smoke, and by the brimstone, which issued out of their mouths. For their power is in their mouth, and in their tails: for their tails were like unto serpents, and had heads, and with them they do hurt (9:16-19).

China, Japan, and India could field this stupendous Army with ease today. Whether a demon-controlled army of human beings or an invasion by the demon world itself, these are irresistible and hellish forces.

Many see symbols of modern warfare described here, including tanks, artillery, and atomic bombs.

The warriors' breastplates are fiery red, blue, and yellow. The lion-headed horses kill with their mouths (fire, smoke, and brimstone as from artillery, armored tanks, or missile launchers) and have serpents with heads for their tails. John may have seen weapons of modern warfare which are capable of projecting rounds of great destruction, including tactical nuclear weapons, for great distances. These events are not far-fetched, because weapons of tremendous destruction are present in the arsenals of most modern nations today. These things are not only possible, but sure, because God said so.

The second woe also includes a great earthquake in Jerusalem in which 7,000 are killed.

> *And the same hour was there a great earthquake, and the tenth part of the city fell, and in the earthquake were slain of men seven thousand: and the remnant were affrighted, and gave glory to the God of heaven. The second woe is past; and, behold, the third woe cometh quickly (11:13-14).*

The earthquake is associated with the "second woe," which we already know is the sixth trumpet. The information is contained in the parenthetical pause between the sixth and seventh trumpets.

There is no peace without the Prince of Peace. The Antichrist, who rode to power on a platform of peace, is unable to deliver. Christ alone can deliver peace.

Unrepentant man (9:20-21)

You would think that by this point in the Great Tribulation men would turn to Christ and repent in droves.

Surely their hearts have melted. Not so –

And the rest of the men which were not killed by these plagues yet repented not of the works of their hands, that they should not worship devils, and idols of gold, and silver, and brass, and stone, and of wood: which neither can see, nor hear, nor walk: neither repented they of their murders, nor of their sorceries, nor of their fornication, nor of their thefts (9:20-21).

What depravity! Those not killed do not repent:
1. Of their evil works and deeds.
2. Of their worship of Satan and demons.
3. Of their worship of idols "which neither can see, nor hear, nor walk." I don't know about you, but I don't want a God I have made myself which can do nothing but sit idly on a shelf.
4. Of their murders.
5. Of their sorceries (*pharmakeion*) — drugs. Drugs will help them endure the judgments and will be part of their religion. They will be so deluded they will accept the Antichrist, who has promised everything and delivered nothing, rather than Christ. Paul wrote about the wicked one, who is the Antichrist, and the delusion of the Great Tribulation:

Even him, whose coming is after the working of Satan, with all power and signs and lying wonders, and with all deceivableness of unrighteousness in them that perish; because they received not the love of the truth, that they might be saved. And for this cause God shall send them strong delusion, that they should believe a lie: that they all might be damned who believed not the truth, but had pleasure in unrighteousness (2 Thess 2:9-12).

    6. Of their fornication — adultery, sexual sins.
    7. Of their thefts — me first, satisfy my wants.

Those who reject Christ will believe the big lies that Satan has always propagated, i.e., that God's Word is not to be trusted, that sin does not result in death, that men can be their own gods, and that humans should by all means satisfy their lusts. Delusion and depravity are deadly. Wicked men will follow the Antichrist with great allegiance and will refuse to repent. The human heart is, indeed, incurably wicked without Christ.

God's Word or Satan's Lie?

Although men can be made to fear God through his judgments, they are not brought to the place of repentance apart from faith in Christ and divine grace. Man apart from God is totally depraved and without hope. The moment you reject the gospel and shut your heart to God, you open yourself to the lies of Satan. Those who stand for nothing will fall for anything every time.

Adam and Eve didn't stand on God's Word, and the race fell. Those who do not stand on the Word today are lost and easy prey for cults. Those who refuse God's Word in the Great Tribulation will not repent. Jesus said, "I am *the* way, *the* truth, and *the* life: no man cometh unto the Father, but by me" (John 14:6), and "For God so loved the world, that he gave his only begotten Son, that whosoever believeth in *him* should not perish, but have everlasting life" (3:16) (italics added). God's Word is the truth. Jesus is the only way.

How about you? Are you standing on God's Word, or are you standing on the lies of Satan? Your answer will determine your destiny. God's Word is always true. It never fails. Satan is the father of lies. It just makes sense to me to trust the Word of God over Satan every time.

Jesus has claimed to be the Son of God and God the Son. The Antichrist will make similar claims. The Antichrist may be Satan incarnate. Satan has always coveted worship. Many will flock to the Antichrist in the Great Tribulation.

If you have not trusted Jesus as your personal Savior, you are as lost as those people will be, and your destiny is the same. That's the truth.

5

BITTERSWEET EXPERIENCE

Revelation 10:1-11

It was March, 1969, and I was in the last stages of Special Forces training. In just a few weeks, I would be a fully qualified Green Beret. At the moment, however, that was the last thing on my mind.

The food I had eaten had been good. The Army said its field rations were good, so I'm sure the food tasted good going down. But those good rations did not agree with my stomach, and I was deathly ill. I didn't have to smell food to throw up; all I had to do was think of food. What had tasted good had become bitter in my stomach.

As I think back on my life, I must admit there have been many experiences that did not turn out just as I thought they would. I have made some poor choices. Some things that seemed so right and so sweet at the time turned out to be so wrong and so bitter. You can identify with that, can't you? So could John. In this chapter, a mighty angel is introduced who has in his possession a little book that

John is commanded to take and eat. Eating the book is for John a bittersweet experience.

It is also possible that some of the most bitter experiences of our lives turn out to be some of the sweetest in retrospect. Sometimes it takes years to understand God's purpose and to taste the honey of life's bitter pills.

Six trumpets have sounded, and one-half of earth's inhabitants have been killed by God's judgments. Some three billion people will have died at the hands of the four horsemen and the army of two hundred million. Rather than repent, however, those on earth continue to reject Christ and to reveal their own depravity. Chapter 10 and much of Chapter 11 of the Revelation are an interlude between the sixth and seventh trumpets, just as Chapter 7 was an interlude between the sixth and seventh seals.

The Mighty Angel and the Seven Thunders (10:1-4)

And I saw another mighty angel come down from heaven, clothed with a cloud: and a rainbow was upon his head, and his face was as it were the sun, and his feet as pillars of fire: and he had in his hand a little book open: and he set his right foot upon the sea, and his left foot on the earth, and cried with a loud voice, as when a lion roareth: and when he had cried, seven thunders uttered their voices. And when the seven thunders had uttered their voices, I was about to write: and I heard a voice from heaven saying unto me, Seal up those things which the seven thunders uttered, and write them not (10:1-4).

The mighty angel (10:1-3a)

This is "another mighty angel" like that of Revelation 5:2 who wondered if anyone in the universe was worthy to open the book. Though he is impressive, this angel is not Christ for at least three reasons.

First, Christ is the preincarnate Angel of the Lord in the Old Testament, but he is the glorified postincarnate Lord in Revelation, never an angel. Before he was born in human form in Bethlehem, Jesus made numerous appearances. These are called theophanies. We only have to think of the fourth man with the three Hebrew boys in the fiery furnace in Babylon to know this is true. He never appeared as an angel after his incarnation.

Second, Christ does not come to earth mid-Tribulation. He comes in the air to take his church out before the Tribulation, but he does not return to earth until he returns in power and glory at the Battle of Armageddon to end the Great Tribulation and establish his earthly kingdom.

Third, the angel swears by one higher than himself, as we shall see in verses five and six. Christ could not swear by one higher, because there is no one higher.

This mighty angel, while not Christ, is special. His clothing of clouds makes clear he is a special envoy from Christ. Angels announced Christ's first coming. This angel announces the second. The rainbow is a reminder of God's covenant. His face shines because he has been in the presence of Christ, as the face of Moses did when he descended from Mt. Sinai. His feet of fire portend coming judgment, because fire speaks of judgment. His pose portrays Christ's ownership of the earth and sea. As Creator and Redeemer, Christ made it and bought it – it belongs to him. His voice is as the roar of a lion, which speaks of majesty and power. He is a special angel.

The little book (10:2a)

The book may be the seven-sealed book, given by the Father, opened by the Son, now transferred to the mighty angel. It is now an "open" book. The seven seals have been opened.

Though not revealed in Scripture, it must contain judgments and authority for the angel's mission. His marching orders are in this little book.

The seven thunders (10:3b-4)

The thunders are God's "Amen" to the angel's claim. The number seven always speaks of completeness. Israel spoke of thunder as being the voice of the Lord. This is likely the voice of Christ confirming that he is about to come to power on earth.

The seven thunders were intelligible. John understood the words he heard and was about to record them when he was forbidden to do so. This part of the Revelation was for John's eyes and ears only. There are secrets which God has not seen fit to reveal to man at this time.

Announcement of the End of the Age (10:5-7)

And the angel which I saw stand upon the sea and upon the earth lifted up his hand to heaven, and sware by him that liveth for ever and ever, who created heaven, and the things that therein are, and the earth, and the things that therein are, and the sea, and the things which are therein, that there should be time no longer: but in the days of the voice of the seventh angel, when he shall begin to sound, the mystery of God should be finished, as he hath declared to his servants the prophets (10:5-7).

The swearing angel (10:5-6b)

Did you know that angels swear? This one does!
If the angel were Christ, he would swear by himself, the Creator.

> *In the beginning was the Word, and the Word was with God, and the Word was God. The same was in the beginning with God. All things were made by him; and without him was not any thing made that was made (John 1:1-3).*

John knew Jesus was the Creator, and so did Paul:

> *For by him were all things created, that are in heaven, and that are in earth, visible and invisible, whether they be thrones, or dominions, or principalities, or powers: all things were created by him, and for him: and he is before all things, and by him all things consist (Col 1:16-17).*

As the representative of Christ, the angel swears by Christ the Creator and claims the universe for Christ.

The answered prayer (10:6b-7)

The martyrs in Revelation 6:10 asked, "How long, O Lord, holy and true, dost thou not judge and avenge our blood on them that dwell on the earth?" The angel announces the delay ("time") is over. Time has run out. The end is to be consummated. The elect are informed it won't be long till Christ returns. "Thy kingdom come" in the Lord's Prayer is about to be answered.
The seventh trumpet will signal the completion of the mystery of God revealed to the Old Testament prophets,

i.e., the glorious return of Christ, establishment of his millennial kingdom, and creation of the eternal state.

Eating of the Little Book (10:8-11)

> *And the voice which I heard from heaven spake unto me again, and said, Go and take the little book which is open in the hand of the angel which standeth upon the sea and upon the earth.*
>
> *And I went unto the angel, and said unto him, Give me the little book. And he said unto me, Take it, and eat it up; and it shall make thy belly bitter, but it shall be in thy mouth sweet as honey. And I took the little book out of the angel's hand, and ate it up; and it was in my mouth sweet as honey: and as soon as I had eaten it, my belly became bitter. And he said unto me, Thou must prophesy again before many peoples, and nations, and tongues, and kings (10:8-11).*

Taking the book (10:8-9)

Christ from Heaven orders John to participate in the drama by taking the book from the angel. It is the same voice that said to John in Revelation 4:1, "Come up hither, and I will shew thee things which must be hereafter."

John goes to the angel and requests the book. The angel instructs John to eat the book, which would be sweet to the taste but bitter to his stomach.

To eat a book is strange (unless you are between the ages of two and three!) but has much meaning. What do you suppose was the purpose of the command to eat? In spy movies, we often see someone eating a note to hide evidence. I believe something more is intended in this case.

Eating the book (10:10-11)

Eating the book means to partake of its contents, to receive by faith God's Word and appropriate its revelations and promises to oneself. As an example, when you got saved, you by faith appropriated the revelation of God and the promises of God in Christ Jesus to yourself. You said, "I believe Jesus Christ died on a cross for me. I claim his death as my death. He died in my place. I believe that he was resurrected for me, and I believe he is coming back for me." Though John ate the book literally, he was symbolically appropriating its contents for himself.

John was not the first in the Bible to eat a book. Jeremiah consumed the Word of God in like manner:

Thy words were found, and I did eat them; and thy word was unto me the joy and rejoicing of mine heart: for I am called by thy name, O Lord God of hosts (Jer 15:16).

Ezekiel did the same thing.

Moreover he said unto me, Son of man, eat that thou findest; eat this roll, and go speak unto the house of Israel. So I opened my mouth, and he caused me to eat that roll. And he said unto me, Son of man, cause thy belly to eat, and fill thy bowels with this roll that I give thee. Then did I eat it; and it was in my mouth as honey for sweetness (Ezek 3:1-3).

God's Word is sweet –

How sweet are thy words unto my taste! yea, sweeter than honey to my mouth (Ps 119:103).

John ate the book. It was sweet in his mouth as God's Word but bitter in his stomach because it spoke of judgment, largely upon Israel, John's nation and countrymen. Christ is sweet, but his judgment is bitter.

Prophecy is sweet, but its applications and demands on our lives can make us bitter.

> *And every man that hath this hope in him purifieth himself, even as he is pure (1 John 3:3).*

Many are more interested in prophecy than in Christian living, some more interested in Antichrist than in Christ. Many want to study what is going to happen in the future without giving a flip about what is happening and how they are living now.

John himself was in bitter straits on Patmos, but God's Words and assurances were sweet to him.

All nations, colors, peoples, and tongues need to be warned judgment is coming. All people on earth will be severely affected by the vision John was given of the Apocalypse. Our mission is not just to present the sweetness of Jesus as a baby in a manger or the sacrifice of Jesus dying on a cross, but also the severity of Jesus judging wickedness and the splendor of Jesus returning in power and glory as the King of kings and Lord of lords.

Bitterness or Sweetness?

The study of prophecy will have a very definite effect upon your life. It will either be sweet to you and draw you closer to Christ, or it will be bitter to you and take you farther from him.

As a lost person, you will either experience the sweetness of accepting Christ as your Savior, or you will continue to know the bitterness of rejecting him.

As a born again Christian, prophecy will either cause you to purify yourself and live a sweet and holy life in light of Christ's imminent return, or it will cause you to stubbornly rebel and live a life of bitterness. You may be bitter today because you refuse to yield to God's clear will for your life in areas such as stewardship, forgiveness, purity, and public identification with the body of Christ in baptism, and you are experiencing God's chastening hand upon your life. If not, you are lost. God's discipline is a sure sign that you are saved. If God does not discipline you, it's because you are not his child. If you are lost, he leaves your discipline to your father, the Devil.

It should be evident to you by now that God is not fooling around. Don't you long for the joy, peace, love, and sweetness of a close relationship and fellowship with Christ? You can have it if you truly want it. Only trust him as your Savior and Lord of your life. When Christ is really Lord of your life, you will know a sweetness you never knew before.

Many things we go through in life do not turn out the way we thought they would. Some are bitter pills to swallow, but later yield such sweetness as we see God's plan at work. Others are sweet to the taste, particularly forbidden fruit, but later yield such bitterness.

God's Word will make us better – or bitter. We must decide whether we will know the sweetness of God or the chastening hand of God. It's easier to do it God's way the first time without the chastening.

6

THE TWO WITNESSES

Revelation 11:1-19

I like cartoons about preachers. So often they give us a rather accurate, if unflattering, view of ourselves as seen by the congregation. I saw one recently in which the preacher in the pulpit said, "Now verse 33 is one of the most controversial verses in all of Scripture, so we're going to skip right over it and go to verse 34."

We're not going to do that with Revelation 11, but if you want to get a good argument going over interpretation of Scripture, this text would be a great place to start. Many try to spiritualize the city, the temple, the witnesses, and the events in the continuing interlude between the sixth and seventh trumpets.

I believe the great city is the literal city of Jerusalem, the time periods are literal time periods, the two witnesses are two individuals, the earthquake is a literal earthquake, the seven thousand who die by the earthquake are literal people, and the death, resurrection, and the ascension of the two witnesses are literal events. I believe those things.

I know your eternal destiny rests in your literal acceptance of the Lord Jesus Christ as your Savior.

The Measuring Rod of God (11:1-2)

> *And there was given me a reed like unto a rod: and the angel stood, saying, Rise, and measure the temple of God, and the altar, and them that worship therein, but the court which is without the temple leave out, and measure it not; for it is given unto the Gentiles: and the holy city shall they tread under foot forty and two months (11:1-2).*

Dealing with Israel (11:1)

John, again an actor, is told to measure the holy place and Holy of holies as well as those who worship therein. In the last chapter he was told to take a little book and eat it. Time and space are not a problem with God, so John, some 1,900 years ago, participated in a drama which has not yet occurred. Put that in your skeptical pipe and smoke it!

The reed is a shepherd's rod used for at least two different things in the Psalms. First, it is an instrument for chastisement and judgment.

> *Thou shalt break them with a rod of iron; thou shalt dash them in pieces like a potter's vessel (Ps 2:9).*

Second, it is a tool for comfort in our times of trouble.

> *Thy rod and thy staff they comfort me (Ps 23:4).*

Measuring is an evaluation of God's property. Jerusalem was measured in Zechariah 2. The kingdom temple was measured in Ezekiel 40. New Jerusalem is measured in Revelation 21.

The temple will be rebuilt and desecrated by the Antichrist, but it, the golden altar of prayer, and the worshippers will be evaluated by God's divine standard. This is not the church, whose bodies (not buildings) are temples. God does not measure the church by the size of the congregation or the size of the building. The Holy Spirit indwells the bodies of believers; our bodies are the temple of the Holy Spirit (1 Corinthians 6:19).

Israel is in view, not the church. It is the time of Jacob's trouble, the purging of Israel, and no amount of spiritualization can make Israel and the church one and the same body.

Times of the Gentiles numbered (11:2)

The outer court is not to be measured. It and Jerusalem will be under Gentile control for another 42 months, the last three and one-half years of the Great Tribulation. Here we have an overview, not the detailed account we find elsewhere, of all that is to come.

This is the last half of Daniel's 70th week. Revelation cannot be understood apart from Daniel. Look at what Daniel said about the Antichrist in the Tribulation:

And he shall speak great words against the most High, and shall wear out the saints of the most High, and think to change times and laws: and they shall be given into his hand until a time and times and the dividing of time (Dan 7:25).

The Lawless One will not only outlaw anything pertaining to Christ, but will also try to change the calendar, no doubt to reflect his own ascendancy and to erase the B.C. and A.D. memorials of Christ's first advent. A "time" is one year, "times" is two, and "the dividing of time" is one-half. That equals three and one-half years.

The Antichrist, who comes on a platform of peace, shows his true colors in the middle of the Tribulation and turns against Israel with full force.

> *And he shall confirm the covenant with many for one week: and in the midst of the week he shall cause the sacrifice and oblation to cease, and for the overspreading of abominations he shall make it desolate, even until the consummation, and that determined shall be poured upon the desolate (Dan 9:27).*

What happens? Antichrist, in the middle of the seven-year Tribulation period, sets himself or his idol up to be worshipped in the Holy of holies. He desecrates the temple of the holy God and halts all sacrifices to the true and living God. It is the abomination of desolation, so the temple is considered desolate.

> *And from the time that the daily sacrifice shall be taken away, and the abomination that maketh desolate set up, there shall be a thousand two hundred and ninety days (Dan 12:11).*

Twelve hundred ninety days from the time Antichrist sets himself up in God's temple to be worshipped until the return of Christ – the time is set.

This time of the Gentiles was also prophesied by the Lord Jesus Christ.

And they shall fall by the edge of the sword, and shall be led away captive into all nations: and Jerusalem shall be trodden down of the Gentiles, until the times of the Gentiles be fulfilled (Luke 21:24).

It is Antichrist's last hurrah:

And there was given unto him a mouth speaking great things and blasphemies; and power was given unto him to continue forty and two months (Rev 13:5).

Forty-two months is three and one-half years, the worst time period the world will have ever experienced.

The times of the Gentiles end at the second coming of Christ when he destroys Gentile control and establishes his kingdom.

The Two Witnesses (11:3-12)

Let's wade right into a controversy, shall we? Who are the two witnesses with such great power identified in this chapter? Do you know? This is fascinating!

Their prophecy (11:3-6)

And I will give power unto my two witnesses, and they shall prophesy a thousand two hundred and threescore days, clothed in sackcloth. These are the two olive trees, and the two candlesticks standing before the God of the earth. And if any man will hurt them, fire proceedeth out of their mouth, and

*devoureth their enemies: and if any man will hurt
them, he must in this manner be killed. These have
the power to shut heaven, that it rain not in the days
of their prophecy: and have power over waters to
turn them to blood, and to smite the earth with all
plagues, as often as they will.*

The 1260 days of prophecy is likely the last half of the
Great Tribulation because the witnesses pour out divine
judgments and need divine protection, which would not
be   necessary in the first half, because the Antichrist
pretends to be a good guy in the first half, a man of peace.
In the last half, he makes no such pretenses, setting
himself up to be worshipped and setting out to destroy
anything related to Christ and every Jew on the earth.

Who are the two witnesses? God did not identify them.
Elijah is almost certainly one of them:

*Behold, I will send you Elijah the prophet before
the coming of the great and dreadful day of the Lord
(Mal 4:5).*

Elijah, of course, was here before the first advent of Christ,
but that was not the "great and dreadful day of the Lord."
The "day of the Lord" begins with the Rapture of the
church and continues through the Great White Throne
judgment of the wicked. It is future, not past.

The other may be Moses, who represents the Law and
was able to bring similar plagues upon Egypt. He also
appeared with Elijah on the Mount of Transfiguration.
Enoch is a possibility, because he did not die, and the
Bible says "it is appointed unto man once to die."   John
the Baptist was the forerunner for the first advent, and
many believe he will be the forerunner for the second
coming. I don't know who they are, and you don't either.

While I am relatively certain Elijah is one of them, it is possible they may be two unknowns.

They are two *human* witnesses by law. They are not Israel, the church, or the Word of God. The Law required two human witnesses, because of the death penalty about to be executed upon so many on the earth:

At the mouth of two witnesses, or three witnesses, shall he that is worthy of death be put to death; but at the mouth of one witness he shall not be put to death (Deut 17:6).

These "olive trees" and "candlesticks" are empowered by the Holy Spirit as in Zechariah 4:6, where Joshua and Zerubbabel stood against insurmountable odds, not in their own strength but in the power and spirit of God.

They are lights in the midst of darkness. They are immortal and immune to attack until their mission is completed. They stop rain, turn water to blood, and bring plagues when they wish. They have the greatest power ever given to any men, exceeding that given to Moses. As you can well imagine, they are a pain in the neck to Antichrist.

Their deaths (11:7-10)

And when they shall have finished their testimony, the beast that ascendeth out of the bottomless pit shall make war against them, and shall overcome them, and kill them. And their dead bodies shall lie in the street of the great city, which spiritually is called Sodom and Egypt, where also our Lord was crucified. And they of the people and kindreds and tongues and nations shall see their dead bodies three days and a half, and shall not suffer their dead bodies to be put in graves. And they that dwell upon the earth shall rejoice over them, and make merry, and shall send gifts one to another; because these two prophets tormented them that dwelt upon the earth (11:7-10).

When their ministry is complete, Satan (or one empowered by him) kills them in Jerusalem, the city "where also our Lord was crucified."

They are treated as animals without decent burial and left exposed for all the world to gaze upon for three and one-half days, likely by television. When I was a child, I wondered how that could be possible. How could everyone in the world see these two bodies? Today, I can tell you the answer without hesitancy. The answer is CNN, ABC, CBS, NBC, and all the other news networks. Within hours we have video of any major event in the world as a result of satellite transmissions. The technology is already in place.

From the very beginning, much controversy has surrounded the resurrection of Christ. Those who won't believe have concocted every explanation imaginable. That will not be the case with the two witnesses. For three and one-half days, the lead story on every network will be, "They are still there!" No doubt CNN Headline News will show them lying in the streets of Jerusalem every half hour. The news anchors will try without success to keep the smirks off their faces as they report the news.

The world rejoices at the "Antichristmas," celebrating what the Antichrist has done. Their insane, inhumane, and hellish glee reveals their hearts. They give gifts to each other, as at Christmas. It will be a worldwide celebration, a mardi gras, an orgy of devilish glee.

The witnesses' deaths diminish not their truths. Killing the messenger does not invalidate the message, any more than crucifying Christ negated the gospel. The truth is still the truth.

Antichristmas is just about to be ruined, however, and the merrymaking about to come to an end.

Their resurrection and ascension (11:11-12)

And after three days and an half the spirit of life from God entered into them, and they stood upon their feet; and great fear fell upon them which saw them. And they heard a great voice from heaven saying unto them, Come up hither. And they ascended up to heaven in a cloud; and their enemies beheld them (11:11-12).

Let's think back to the television news coverage for a moment. No empty tomb this time! No controversy, no doubt, no swoon theories, no stolen body explanations, no missing this resurrection.

"Dateline: Jerusalem – Troublemakers Resurrected!" The merrymaking ends suddenly. As the world watches, the two are raised from the dead. A great voice calls from Heaven, and they ascend in a cloud of glory in full view as Christ did, but seen by the whole world. What a stunning development.

"Antichristmas" will be ruined!

The Seventh Trumpet (11:13-19)

The resurrection and ascension of the two witnesses is not without a convulsion in nature. God shakes Jerusalem with a "great earthquake" to add his exclamation mark to the day's events. The parenthetical interlude between the sixth and seventh trumpets comes to an end, and the seventh trumpet (third "woe" trumpet) signals the continuation of judgments upon an unbelieving and unrepentant world.

Announcement of the third woe (11:13-14)

And the same hour was there a great earthquake, and the tenth part of the city fell, and in the earthquake were slain of men seven thousand: and the remnant were affrighted, and gave glory to the God of heaven. The second woe is past; and, behold, the third woe cometh quickly (11:13-14).

An earthquake shakes Jerusalem as at Christ's death (Matthew 27:51-52) and resurrection (Matthew 28:2). Seven thousand die; the others fearfully glorify God but probably do not by faith trust Christ. If "remnant" speaks of the Jewish remnant, it may well be that many trust Christ because of the witness of the two prophets and the events surrounding their death and resurrection.

This ends the second woe; the third soon begins.

The seventh trumpet sounds (11:15-19)

And the seventh angel sounded; and there were great voices in heaven, saying, The kingdoms of this world are become the kingdoms of our Lord, and of his Christ; and he shall reign for ever and ever. And the four and twenty elders, which sat before God on their seats, fell upon their faces, and worshipped God, saying, We give thee thanks, O Lord God Almighty, which art, and wast, and art to come; because thou hast taken to thee thy great power, and hast reigned. And the nations were angry, and thy wrath is come, and the time of the dead, that they should be judged, and that thou shouldest give reward unto thy servants the prophets, and to the saints, and them that fear thy name, small and great; and shouldest destroy them which destroy the earth. And the temple of God was opened in heaven, and there was seen in his temple the ark of his testament: and there were lightnings, and voices, and thunderings, and an earthquake, and great hail (11:15-19).

The seventh trumpet is of utmost significance as an overview of all that is to follow. It includes the vials of wrath, the second coming of Christ, and the millennial reign. It continues to the beginning of eternity. All of the rest of time is included in the seventh trumpet.

Great voices jubilantly announce Christ's triumph over evil and assumption of authority over the kingdom of the world. Never again will Satan or man have control or rule.

The elders (church) celebrate prayers answered: "Thy kingdom come. Thy will be done in earth, as it is in heaven" (Matt 6:10). Christ will rule with absolute authority during the millennium.

The nations are angry at God's wrath — angry and wrath are the same word. The wrath of man is impotent and evil; the wrath of God is omnipotent and holy. I believe God will laugh at the impotent anger of wicked men. Rather than repent, they shake their fists in God's face.

The Great White Throne judgment of the wicked and reward of Old Testament and tribulation saints are in view.

The earthly temple may be desecrated, but the heavenly temple reflects righteousness and majesty. The ark speaks of God's sure covenants. I love Indiana Jones movies. Several years ago, one such film was entitled, "Raiders of the Lost Ark." It's theme was a search for the Ark of the Covenant. In the movie, "Indy" found it. In reality, the Ark is apparently in Heaven and probably still contains the tablets of stone, Aaron's rod that budded, and the bowl of manna.

Lightnings, voices, thunderings, earthquake, and hail all speak of God's summary judgment that will culminate in Christ's return in power and glory at Armageddon.

Is Your Time Almost Up?

Forty-two months the Gentiles will have left. Forty-two months the two witnesses will prophesy. Forty-two months God's wrath will be poured out on the sinful earth. Then Jesus will return in power and glory.

Dominion is his by divine decree. No one will escape him. No one will go around him. Everyone will acknowledge him as Lord. Everyone will agree that he is indeed "the way, the truth, and the life," and, yes, that nobody can come to the Father but by him. Everyone who has ever lived will acknowledge that Jesus is Lord.

What about you? Have you accepted Jesus as Savior and Lord? How much time do you have left? Is it 42 months, 42 weeks, 42 days, 42 hours, 42 minutes, or 42 seconds? None of us know. But we do know we'll answer to Jesus when our time is up. Are you ready?

Jesus wants to be your Savior. If not, he will be your Judge. He is the Lord.

7

WAR IN HEAVEN AND EARTH

Revelation 12:1-17

The seventh trumpet of Revelation 11 introduces all the events and judgments leading to the Second Coming of Christ in chapter 19. There is almost more information than we can digest. I pray that God will give you a cup of understanding big enough to grasp the entirety of the seventh trumpet.

Time is very short for mankind on earth, and the judgments come rapidly. John now fills in some of the details by introducing in this chapter and the next seven personages who play an important role in the Great Tribulation. The events of Revelation 12 and 13 are concurrent with the seals and trumpets, not chronological at any given point.

In this chapter, we will discover a woman, a red dragon, a man child, an archangel, and a remnant. One of the five is the key to interpretation of the entire Book of

Revelation. When you understand who that person is, you will know how to interpret the book.

The Woman and the Dragon (12:1-4)

The best way to digest all the information in this chapter is to take it a bite at a time, chew it thoroughly, swallow it, and chase it with a large gulp of discernment from the Holy Spirit. Let's try that.

The Woman: Israel (12:1-2)

And there appeared a great wonder in heaven; a woman clothed with the sun, and the moon under her feet, and upon her head a crown of twelve stars: and she being with child cried, travailing in birth, and pained to be delivered (12:1-2).

I won't keep you in suspense as to which of the persons is the key to Revelation. Your interpretation of the woman will determine your interpretation of prophecy and Revelation. Who is the woman?

The Catholics say the woman is the Virgin Mary. Many Protestants say she is the church. Some female cult leaders have identified themselves – big of them, isn't it? None of those are true nor can be true.

The woman is a sign in heaven, a reality on earth. A sign is a symbol.

Her identifying marks are the sun, moon, and stars. Do you remember in the Bible where the sun, moon, and stars identify a people? It's in the Bible's first book. These belong to Israel: Jacob, Rachel, and the patriarchs, sons of Jacob. Think back to the dream of Joseph, which he foolishly shared with his less than thrilled brothers. It was a prophetic dream.

And he dreamed yet another dream, and told it his brethren, and said, Behold, I have dreamed a dream more; and behold, the sun and the moon and the eleven stars made obeisance to me. And he told it to his father and to his brethren: and his father rebuked him, and said unto him, What is this dream that thou hast dreamed? Shall I and thy mother and thy brethren indeed come to bow down ourselves to thee to the earth? (Gen 37:9-10).

Did you see it? Jacob is the sun, Rachel the moon, and the stars are the tribes of Israel. This is the only place in Scripture where a people are identified in such a manner.

Israel gave birth to Christ, who is the child. Her travail continues after the birth of the child, according to Isaiah's prophecy, as Israel will go through the Great Tribulation after the birth of Christ. No woman (Mary or cult leaders) fits this description, nor does the church. Travail, or labor pains, normally end with delivery. Not so, Israel, who suffers through labor pains *after* delivery of the child:

Before she travailed, she brought forth; before her pain came, she was delivered of a man child. Who hath heard such a thing? Who hath seen such things? Shall the earth be made to bring forth in one day? or shall a nation be born at once? for as soon as Zion travailed, she brought forth her children (Isa 66:7-8).

The woman is Israel. Israel's labor pains are yet to come.

The red dragon: Satan (12:3-4)

And there appeared another wonder in heaven; and behold a great red dragon, having seven heads and ten horns, and seven crowns upon his heads.

And his tail drew the third part of the stars of heaven, and did cast them to the earth: and the dragon stood before the woman which was ready to be delivered, for to devour her child as soon as it was born (12:3-4).

This is also a sign or symbol. It is not literal. The dragon is identified as Satan in Revelation 12:9, so this was easy. He is called "great" because of his power and control of the world. He desires worship. He is called "red" because he is a murderer. He is called a "dragon" because he is vicious.

Seven heads speak of complete wisdom. Again, we must go to the Old Testament.

Son of man, take up a lamentation upon the king of Tyrus, and say unto him, Thus saith the Lord God; Thou sealest up the sum, full of wisdom, and perfect in beauty (Ezek 28:12).

The king of Tyrus is Satan, who is full of wisdom. He can deceive you in many ways. You cannot possibly fight him successfully in your own strength or intelligence.

Ten horns refer to the revived Roman Empire with which he tries to rule the world. Again, our research takes us to the Old Testament.

After this, I saw in the night visions, and behold a fourth beast, dreadful and terrible, and strong exceedingly; and it had great iron teeth: it devoured and brake in pieces, and stamped the residue with the feet of it: and it was diverse from all the beasts that were before it; and it had ten horns.

I considered the horns, and, behold, there came up among them another little horn, before whom there were three of the first horns plucked up by the roots: and behold, in this horn were eyes like the eyes of man, and a mouth speaking great things.

And the ten horns out of this kingdom are ten kings that shall arise: and another shall rise after them; and he shall be diverse from the first, and shall subdue three kings (Dan 7:7-8, 24).

You recognize, of course, that Antichrist is the little horn who subdues three kings and thus gains control over the 10 nations as the majority party. Antichrist is Satan's man, and we will learn much more about him later.

A third of the stars of Heaven reflect Satan's forces of angels that followed him in rebellion. A third of the holy angels became fallen angels in an instant when they decided to follow Lucifer in his quest to be God.

He is seen awaiting the birth of the child to kill it, as he tried to do by Herod, an Edomite (son of Esau). This was predicted by God in the first pronouncement of the gospel, made to Lucifer himself:

And I will put enmity between thee and the woman, and between thy seed and her seed; it shall bruise thy head, and thou shalt bruise his heel (Gen 3:15).

The Child and the Archangel (12:5-12)

The woman is Israel. The red dragon is Satan. Now let's identify the child of the woman and the archangel who fights the dragon. The child is the most important person who has ever lived, and he is from Israel. I'll just bet you've already figured out who he is, this man child whom Satan wanted to kill so badly.

The man child: Christ (12:5-6)

> *And she brought forth a man child, who was to rule all nations with a rod of iron: and her child was caught up unto God, and to his throne. And the woman fled into the wilderness, where she hath a place prepared of God, that they should feed her there a thousand two hundred and threescore days (12:5-6).*

The child is clearly Christ, who will rule all nations with a rod of iron.

> *Thou shalt break them with a rod of iron; thou shalt dash them in pieces like a potter's vessel (Ps 2:9).*

> *And out of his mouth goeth a sharp sword, that with it he should smite the nations: and he shall rule them with a rod of iron: and he treadeth the winepress of the fierceness and wrath of Almighty God (Rev 19:15).*

He puts down rebellion with power, not pacifism. He rules actively, not passively. He rules righteously, not permissively.

He was "caught up" in his ascension. The Book of Revelation depends on the ascended Christ who is unveiled in his glory. He's at the throne.

Verse 6 "fast forwards" to the Great Tribulation. A remnant of Israel (the woman) will flee into the wilderness and be divinely protected for three and one-half years at an unnamed place, which some believe to be the rock-hewn city of Petra. God always has a remnant. The "time of Jacob's trouble" will be no different.

The archangel: Michael (12:7-9)

And there was war in heaven: Michael and his angels fought against the dragon; and the dragon fought and his angels, and prevailed not; neither was their place found any more in heaven. And the great dragon was cast out, that old serpent, called the Devil, and Satan, which deceiveth the whole world: he was cast out into the earth, and his angels were cast out with him (12:7-9).

Michael and Gabriel are the only archangels named in the Bible, but there may be more. Michael's ministry is with Israel. Daniel wrote of a prayer personally answered by an angel who had been delayed 21 days by a chieftain in the hierarchy of demons. Michael, who had oversight of Israel, came to the angel's aid. The angel told Daniel,

But the prince of the kingdom of Persia withstood me one and twenty days: but, lo, Michael, one of the chief princes, came to help me; . . . (Dan 10:13a).

Just because we do not see demons does not mean there is not a spiritual warfare being fought. Michael is always associated with Israel and is her defender.

As the accuser, Satan has access to Heaven. It may surprise you to know that Satan is not now locked up in Hell. It may distress you to know that he accuses you before the throne of God, just as he accused Job. It may thrill you to know that Jesus is your defense attorney who pleads his blood on your behalf.

Note the descriptive terms given here for Satan:

    1. "That old serpent," from the garden of Eden.

    2. "Devil," slanderer or accuser, the source of malicious gossip, the reason I need an Advocate.

3. "Satan," adversary or enemy.
4. "He that deceiveth the whole world," which he
   will do in the Great Tribulation.

The Devil and his angels are finally expelled from Heaven in a tremendous war.

> *And at that time shall Michael stand up, the great prince which standeth for the children of thy people: and there shall be a time of trouble, such as never was since there was a nation even to that same time: and at that time thy people shall be delivered, every one that shall be found written in the book (Dan 12:1).*

The victory (12:10-12)

> *And I heard a great voice saying in heaven, Now is come salvation, and strength, and the kingdom of our God, and the power of his Christ: for the accuser of our brethren is cast down, which accused them before our God day and night. And they overcame him by the blood of the Lamb, and by the word of their testimony; and they loved not their lives unto the death. Therefore rejoice, ye heavens, and ye that dwell in them. Woe to the inhabiters of the earth and of the sea! for the devil is come down unto you, having great wrath, because he knoweth that he hath but a short time (12:10-12).*

Satan's expulsion causes Heaven to rejoice. The consummation of salvation, the manifested power of Christ, and the establishment of his kingdom are all at hand.

The accused saints will be victorious for three reasons. First, the blood of Jesus Christ nullifies Satan's accusations. Second, the true gospel nullifies Satan's deceit. Third, the death of a saint nullifies Satan's power. What a rush it must be to thumb your nose at the Devil as you pass from this life to the next in the ultimate victory over his most powerful weapon! Those who are taken alive in the Rapture will miss the experience of trusting Jesus Christ all the way to and through physical death.

Heaven rejoices, but the earth trembles, because Satan knows his confinement is close at hand. He can read the Bible, and he is aware he will be bound for 1,000 years, released for a short time to lead his final rebellion, and then consigned to the lake of fire for all eternity. His verdict was sure at the death, burial, and resurrection of Christ. He angrily faces the prospect of the sentence being executed. He will not be a happy camper!

The Persecution and Intervention (12:13-17)

We have seen Israel, Satan, Christ, and Michael the archangel as the first four personages in this overview of the Great Tribulation. Now we will see Satan going ballistic against Israel before we are introduced to the fifth personage, the Jewish remnant.

The persecution of Israel (12:13)

> *And when the dragon saw that he was cast unto the earth, he persecuted the woman which brought forth the man child (12:13).*

Anti-Semitism will reach its highest level ever. Satan hates Israel because she is God's chosen people and essential to God's purpose. He will have no mercy on the nation which brought forth his ultimate foe, the Lord Jesus Christ.

Jews are even today flocking to Israel, thinking they are heading to Palestine for the Millennium. First, however, comes the Tribulation. That's why they are being gathered in Palestine.

The intervention of God (12:14-16)

And to the woman were given two wings of a great eagle, that she might fly into the wilderness, into her place, where she is nourished for a time, and times, and half a time, from the face of the serpent. And the serpent cast out of his mouth water as a flood after the woman, that he might cause her to be carried away of the flood. And the earth helped the woman, and the earth opened her mouth, and swallowed up the flood which the dragon cast out of his mouth (12:14-16).

Wings of an eagle speak of God's grace (Exodus 19:4), not airplane wings. God brought Israel out of Egypt "on eagles' wings," or on the wings of his grace. God will take care of Israel again by his grace.

God has a place where the remnant will be supernaturally sheltered and fed for 42 months, not unlike his divine care of Israel the 40 years in the wilderness. It is one thing to flee and find shelter, but another thing altogether to be fed for three and one-half years.

The place is not identified, but is literal. Jesus said it was in the mountains:

Then let them which be in Judea flee into the mountains (Matt 24:16).

God delivered Israel out of water at the Red Sea and the Jordan River, so this deluge from Satan could be literal water.   It could also be a flood of armies trying to overwhelm them. Don't believe me? Check this out:

Now therefore, behold, the Lord bringeth up upon them the waters of the river, strong and many, even the king of Assyria, and all his glory: and he shall come up over all his channels, and go over all his banks: and he shall pass through Judah; he shall overflow and go over, he shall reach even to the neck; and the stretching out of his wings shall fill the breadth of thy land, O Immanuel (Isa 8:7-8).

The Assyrian army was called a flood. Whatever flood means in Revelation, God supernaturally intervenes, opens up the earth to swallow the flood, and thwarts Satan's attempts to destroy Israel.

The remnant of Jewish believers (12:17)

And the dragon was wroth with the woman, and went to make war with the remnant of her seed, which keep the commandments of God, and have the testimony of Jesus Christ (12:17).

Satan's wrath is particulary hot against the Jews who accept Christ. The "remnant of her seed" is probably the 144,000 sealed witnesses who are evangelizing the world in spite of Satan. Satan cannot kill the 144,000. They are a thorn in his flesh as they lead millions to trust Christ.

Satan will so hate the Jews and will lead the world in such an anti-Semitic movement that two-thirds of all Jews will be killed.

And it shall come to pass, that in all the land, saith the Lord, two parts therein shall be cut off and die; but the third part shall be left therein. And I will bring the third part through the fire, and will refine them as silver is refined, and will try them as gold is tried: they shall call on my name, and I will hear them: I will say, It is my people: and they shall say, the Lord is my God (Zech 13:8-9).

God will divinely protect and nourish the remnant, refining them in the process and preparing them for the Millennium. A third will survive while two-thirds die at the hands of an angry Devil.

Satan the Accuser vs. Jesus the Victor

All anti-Semitism is inspired by Satan and will culminate in his making a final, supreme effort to destroy the nation of Israel. From Pharaoh's brickyards in Egypt, Haman's gallows, Herod's edict, and Hitler's holocaust, to the hell of the Great Tribulation, Satan has tried to destroy the Israelites because of the man child, Jesus Christ.

Why would he go to so much trouble for so long? Only because he knows that Jesus Christ sealed his defeat at the cross of Calvary. The fatal blow has been struck, but Satan will go down fighting. Every time a soul is redeemed by the blood of the Lamb, Jesus Christ, Satan loses another round.

Whose corner are you in — Satan the accuser or Jesus the victor? Satan knows he is going to lose, and he wants to take you down with him. The choice is yours: win with Jesus, or lose with Satan. Won't you be a winner?

$$8$$

THE TWO BEASTS

Revelation 13:1-18

For you, this may well be the most fascinating part of the Revelation. It is for many people. Some spend their entire lives trying to put a name to Antichrist. I can only say, "Good luck!"

The mark of the beast and his number, 666, intrigue us.

The last two personages to be introduced by the seventh trumpet are the Antichrist and the False Prophet. One is described as the beast out of the sea and the other as the beast out of the earth. One is political, the other religious. Along with Satan, the red dragon, they form an unholy trinity which imitates the holy trinity of Father, Son, and Holy Ghost.

To be anti-Christ means to either be an enemy or an imitator of Christ. The beast out of the sea is the white horse rider who tries to imitate Christ. The beast out of the earth denies the deity of Christ and ascribes deity to the first beast; thus, he is against Christ. Both of these beasts, then, can be correctly called anti-Christ, as can Satan, the one who gives them power.

The Beast Out of the Sea (13:1-10)

And I stood upon the sand of the sea, and saw a beast rise up out of the sea, having seven heads and ten horns, and upon his horns ten crowns, and upon his heads the name of blasphemy. And the beast which I saw was like unto a leopard, and his feet were as the feet of a bear, and his mouth as the mouth of a lion: and the dragon gave him his power, and his seat, and great authority. And I saw one of his heads as it were wounded to death; and his deadly wound was healed: and all the world wondered after the beast. And they worshipped the dragon which gave power unto the beast: and they worshipped the beast, saying, Who is like unto the beast? Who is able to make war with him?

And there was given unto him a mouth speaking great things and blasphemies; and power was given unto him to continue forty and two months. And he opened his mouth in blasphemy against God, to blaspheme his name, and his tabernacle, and them that dwell in heaven. And it was given unto him to make war with the saints, and to overcome them: and power was given him over all kindreds, and tongues, and nations. And all that dwell upon the earth shall worship him, whose names are not written in the book of life of the Lamb slain from the foundation of the world.

If any man have an ear, let him hear. He that leadeth into captivity shall go into captivity: he that killeth with the sword must be killed with the sword. Here is the patience and the faith of the saints (13:1-10).

Description: political (13:1-2)

Satan now gets what he has always wanted, full control of the earth, but he will fail. He brings forth his masterpiece, the wild beast out of the sea of humanity and the Mediterranean. The word "sea" in the Bible may speak of either humanity or the Mediterranean; here it speaks of both.

This beast is both a person and a system, the revived Roman Empire. He's the "little horn" of Daniel 7:8, the Man of Sin, and world dictator.

Seven speaks of completeness. Seven heads speak of complete wisdom. His seven heads represent the remnant of the Roman Empire, an imitation of the omniscience of Christ, and blasphemy (making oneself equal with God and slandering God).

The ten horns and crowns speak of the tenfold division of the revived Roman Empire and the kings who rule ten nations. The interpretation is given to us in Revelation 17.

And the ten horns which thou sawest are ten kings, which have received no kingdom as yet; but receive power as kings one hour with the beast (Rev 17:12).

"One hour" means a short period of time.

His kingdom will have all the characteristics of the Babylonian, Greek, Media-Persian, and Roman empires. To understand these, it is necessary to again visit our friend Daniel in the Old Testament. I just imagine Daniel and John have had plenty to talk about for the past 1,900 years or so. Both received great end-time revelations.

Daniel describes the world's greatest empires. The first is the mighty Babylonian empire of Nebuchadnezzar which Daniel saw first hand:

> *And four great beasts came up from the sea, diverse one from another.*
>
> *The first was like a lion, and had eagle's wings: I beheld till the wings thereof were plucked, and it was lifted up from the earth, and made stand upon the feet as a man, and a man's heart was given to it (Dan 7:3-4).*

The second is the Media-Persia empire:

> *And I beheld another beast, a second, like to a bear, and it raised up itself on one side, and it had three ribs in the mouth of it between the teeth of it: and they said thus unto it, Arise, devour much flesh (Dan 7:5).*

The third is the Greek empire under Alexander the Great:

> *After this I beheld, and lo another, like a leopard, which had upon the back of it four wings of a fowl; the beast had also four heads, and dominion was given to it (Dan 7:6).*

The fourth is the Roman empire:

> *After this I saw in the night visions, and behold a fourth beast, dreadful and terrible, and strong exceedingly; and it had great iron teeth: it devoured and brake in pieces, and stamped the residue with the feet of it: and it was diverse from all the beasts that were before it; and it had ten horns (Dan 7:7).*

The fifth is the revived Roman empire of Antichrist, the "little horn":

> *I considered the horns, and, behold, there came up among them another little horn, before whom there were three of the first horns plucked up by the roots: and, behold, in this horn were eyes like the eyes of man, and a mouth speaking great things (Dan 4:8).*
>
> *Thus he said, The fourth beast shall be the fourth kingdom upon earth, which shall be diverse from all kingdoms, and shall devour the whole earth, and shall tread it down, and break it into pieces. And the ten horns out of this kingdom are ten kings that shall arise: and another shall rise after them; and he shall be diverse from the first, and he shall subdue three kings. And he shall speak great words against the most High, and shall wear out the saints of the most High, and think to change times and laws: and they shall be given into his hand until a time and times and the dividing of time (Dan 7:23-25).*

Sounds like Daniel and John got their material from the same source, doesn't it? Antichrist will arise from among the 10 kings, will subdue three, and will gain majority control. He will be allowed to dominate the earth for three and one-half years.

Antichrist is probably the incarnation of Satan himself, just as Jesus was God incarnate. He will be as perfect an imitation of Christ as Satan can manage.

Deity: assumed (13:3-4)

Many have tried to identify Antichrist as Nero, Judas Iscariot, Mussolini, Hitler, or Stalin. In recent years, cases have been made for Henry Kissinger and Ronald Wilson Reagan (six letters in each name equals 666!). Many have been identified as Antichrist. Not one was.

Though Satan cannot raise the dead, this man and system will appear to be resurrected from death. The Roman Empire has been long dormant, but it will be revived as if from the dead. Antichrist himself will appear to be resurrected from a deadly wound, so complete will his imitation of Christ be.

Here's the sad part. Ungodly men won't worship the resurrected Christ, but they will worship the "resurrected" Antichrist and his father, Satan, who finally gets the worship he has always coveted.

Defiance: proclaimed (13:5-8)

Antichrist will be charasmatic but blasphemous. He blasphemes God, the name of God, tabernacle of God, and saints and angels of God. Anything godly becomes a target for his venom. He is Satan's irreverent mouthpiece.

His satanic power is worldwide to kill all who do not worship him. All will worship him, except those whose names are in the Lamb's book of life.

For 42 months he achieves what others have only dreamed about: world domination. He will have power that no one else has every had upon the earth.

Defense: impossible (13:9-10)

Those with spiritual ears – or hearing aids – should know that resistance against the beast is futile. If you are tuned in to the Holy Spirit and have spiritual discernment, you should take note of this.

Martyrdom will be the "patience and the faith" of the saints during the Great Tribulation. True saints will demonstate their faith by enduring the deprivation, torture, and death that is their fate, reckoning with Paul "that the sufferings of this present time are not worthy to be compared to the glory which shall be revealed in us" (Romans 8:18).

The world will be Satan's during this time. The Holy Spirit will not restrain him. Most will fall for Satan's lies.

The spiritual ear would also understand that divine retribution will come shortly.

The Beast Out of the Earth (13:11-18)

And I beheld another beast coming up out of the earth; and he had two horns like a lamb, and he spake as a dragon. And he exerciseth all the power of the first beast before him, and causeth the earth and them which dwell therein to worship the first beast, whose deadly wound was healed. And he doeth great wonders, so that he maketh fire come down from heaven on the earth in the sight of men, and deceiveth them that dwell on the earth by the means of those miracles which he had power to do in the sight of the beast: saying to them that dwell on the earth that they should make an image to the beast, which had the wound by a sword, and did live. And he had power to give life unto the image of the beast, that the image of the beast should both speak, and cause that as many as would not worship the image of the beast should be killed. And he causeth all, both small and great, rich and poor, free and bond, to receive a mark in their right hand, or in their foreheads: and that no man might buy or sell, save he that had the mark, or the name of the beast, or the number of his name.

Here is wisdom. Let him that hath understanding count the number of the beast: for it is the number of a man; and his number is Six hundred and three score and six (13:11-19).

Description: religious (13:11)

Whereas the beast out of the sea was political, this beast comes out of the earth (Palestine) as a lamb, or false messiah and religious prophet. He is the False Prophet.

As a Jew, he will be accepted by the Jews. Many believe he, and possibly the first beast, will come from the apostate tribe of Dan.

He is the epitome of false prophets. He looks like a lamb, but inside he is something far different. Jesus described such pretenders, when he said,

> *Beware of false prophets, which come to you in sheep's clothing, but inwardly they are ravening wolves (Matt 7:15).*

The False Prophet speaks by the power of Satan, the dragon. His appearance as a lamb is inviting and warm. His identity as the Devil's mouthpiece is repulsive and cold. As is true with any false prophet, he is not what he appears. He is religious but demon-possessed and demon-controlled.

Deception: miraculous(13:12-14)

Just as the Holy Spirit is equal with the Father and Son, so this beast has equal satanic power with Antichrist. This unholy trinity is an imitation of the holy trinity. Satan, Antichrist, and the False Prophet portray themselves as the the holy trinity of Father, Son (Christ), and Holy Spirit. The deception is so convincing that most people on earth during the Great Tribulation will worship them.

The False Prophet exalts the first beast and mimics Elijah on Mt. Carmel and the Holy Spirit on the Day of

Pentecost by bringing down fire from heaven. He displays power to match that of a great Old Testament prophet and of the Holy Spirit in founding the New Testament church. Many will wrongly assume he is the Holy Spirit. He is, in fact, the unholy spirit.

The world believes his miracles. It is very, very dangerous to believe in miracles alone! Many of those who followed Jesus Christ during his first advent believed on him for the miracles which he performed, but they never trusted him by faith as the Messiah. They thrilled to the thousands fed, the dead raised, the hurting healed, the water turned into wine. The same will be true as the world flocks after the miracle-working False Prophet. If you doubt this, take a look at the throngs who follow so-called miracle-working TV evangelists today.

Be very careful about falling for miracles, because Satan has great power, and he can perform miracles, too. He can make you sick and then take the sickness away at just the right time ("Place your hand on the radio and feel the power!"), making it appear you were healed. Hello!

The False Prophet causes an image of the first beast to be made and placed in the Jerusalem temple as the center of false worship and focal point of the final state of apostasy. This is the abomination of desolation spoken of by Daniel the prophet. Jesus, the New Testament mercy seat exalted by the Holy Spirit, is replaced in the Holy of holies by the Antichrist exalted by the False Prophet. What an abomination! What a desecration! What a despicable act by Satan, who covets worship, but who can only receive worship under false pretenses.

Delusion: perpetrated (13:15-17)

The False Prophet will have the power to give breath (*pneuma*) and speech to the image. Whether real or fake, the world will fall for it. "Wow! Look at that! What power! What miracles! Antichrist must be the Son of God!"

Politics, religion, and business will now all be combined. Can you imagine the power of one who could control world politics, religion, and business? The religious beast causes worship of the political beast and business identification by the mark of the beast. Satan exercises complete control through his Antichrist.

The mark is a token of beast worship, necessary to purhase the necessities of life, and a device to force all people to worship the beast. The mark may be the name or number of the beast.

I almost never use a credit card. I use a debit card, which subtracts money from my checking account at the time of purchase. When I have no more money in the account, I lose my power to buy. I am identified by a magnetic strip on the back of the card. That strip contains my name and account number and God only knows what else. It is very convenient to use.

The question is, why do I need a card at all? Wouldn't it be easier to have a mark, perhaps invisible, in the hand or forehead? Then I would not need to carry a card or any other identification. I could be instantly scanned and identified anywhere on earth if the system were in place. In the Tribulation, the system will be in place.

We sometimes sing, "I'd rather have Jesus than silver or gold. I'd rather have Jesus than houses or land." Oh, really? Do you love your children enough to let them starve to death? Could you watch your child starve to death when food is available with the mark? Do you love your wife or husband enough to let him or her starve to death? Would you be homeless and penniless for Jesus?

Mothers and fathers will make that decision in the Great Tribulation. "I'd rather have Jesus than anything this world affords today." That's easy to sing on Sunday morning in a church worship service. It'll be a gut-wrenching decision for millions during the Great Tribulation when it really counts. Would you really rather have Jesus than your next meal – or any meal at all?

Not to receive the mark of the beast in the right hand or forehead means physical death; to receive the mark is the Great Tribulation's unpardonable sin and means spiritual death, i.e., separation from God forever:

> *And the third angel followed them, saying with a loud voice, If any man worship the beast, and his image, and receive his mark in his forehead, or in his hand, the same shall drink of the wine of the wrath of God, which is poured out without mixture into the cup of his indignation; and he shall be tormented with fire and brimstone in the presence of the holy angels, and in the presence of the Lamb (Rev 14:9-10).*

Designation: number (13:18)

The number of the beast is 666, the number of man with each digit falling short of a perfect seven. Satan's best still falls short of God's glory. He can never measure up! He can never be a seven!

I believe you can make anyone's name add up to 666 in some language if you try hard enough. Many live to identify Antichrist. Every generation names someone.

Talk about an exercise in futility. This is one of them. It is useless to speculate as to whom 666 designates, because he cannot be revealed until the Great Tribulation Period. The Holy Spirit must be removed as a restraint first. Paul wrote this to the Thessalonians:

Now we beseech you, brethren, by the coming of our Lord Jesus Christ, and by our gathering together unto him, that ye be not soon shaken in mind, or be troubled, neither by spirit, nor by word, nor by letter as from us, as that the day of Christ is at hand.

Let no man deceive you by any means: for that day shall not come, except there come a falling away first, and that man of sin be revealed, the son of perdition; who opposeth and exalteth himself above all that is called God, or that is worshipped; so that he as God sitteth in the temple of God, shewing himself that he is God.

Remember ye not, that, when I was yet with you, I told you these things? And now ye know what withholdeth that he might be revealed in his time. For the mystery of iniquity doth already work: only he who now letteth will let, until he be taken out of the way. And then shall that Wicked be revealed, whom the Lord shall consume with the spirit of his mouth, and shall destroy with the brightness of his coming: even him, whose coming is after the working of Satan with all power and signs and lying wonders, and with all deceivableness of unrighteousness in them that perish; because they received not the love of the truth, that they might be saved.

And for this cause God shall send them strong delusion, that they should believe a lie: that they all might be damned who believed not the truth, but had pleasure in unrighteousness (2 Thess 2:1-12).

Sounds like Paul and John were in touch with the same source, also, doesn't it? The Antichrist cannot possibly be revealed until the Holy Spirit is removed. The Holy Spirit currently makes his abode in the bodies of believers. Only when the church is taken out and the Holy Spirit removes himself from a restraining role ("letteth" in verse 7 means "hinders"), can the "Wicked" or "Wicked One" be revealed (verse 8).

Oh, by the way, many believe that Judas Iscariot resurrected is the Antichrist because both are called "the son of perdition." Again, we just do not know, but it makes an interesting argument.

Whose Mark Do You Bear?

You may want to know more about Antichrist and the False Prophet, but this chapter makes me want to know more about Jesus Christ. You can stick around and find out who Antichrist is if you want to, but I'll be spending the Great Tribulation in Heaven with the Lord Jesus Christ.

Satan will rule the world and be worshipped. False religion and evil will sweep the earth. Man will not be able to solve his own problems, and Antichrist's rule will end in chaos and world war.

Whereas Christ patiently knocks at the heart's door with the truth of the gospel, the unholy trinity of Satan, Antichrist, and the unholy spirit (False Prophet) will deceive and force men to worship them. I don't believe contrived worship counts for much. Those who will not accept the free offer of God's grace and the mark of his blood will in that day accept the costly and damning mark of the beast.

All will be revealed. Everyone will either wear the uniform of Christ or the uniform of Antichrist. There'll be no secret believers or secret beast worshippers. With whom are you identified?

You cannot sit on the fence. You are either with Christ or against Christ.

Whose mark do you bear?

9

VICTORY OF THE LAMB

Revelation 14:1-20

The seventh seal introduced the seven trumpets. The seventh trumpet introduced the seven personalities: the woman, Israel; the red dragon, Satan; the man child, Christ; the archangel, Michael; the Jewish remnant; the beast out of the sea, Antichrist; and the beast out of the earth, the False Prophet.

This text is an interlude between the seven personalities and the seven vials of wrath. As an interlude, it breaks the pattern by coming after the seventh in the series, not the sixth, because the sixth and seventh persons, Antichrist and the False Prophet, had to be considered together. The progression is, as expected, very orderly.

Revelation 14 is packed with critical information. We will see the Lamb on Mount Zion and hear the everlasting gospel proclaimed. Judgment upon Babylon and those who receive the mark of the Beast is pronounced, as is praise for those that die in the Lord. We will preview the ultimate victory of Christ at Armageddon.

How will God's people on earth fare during the Great Tribulation Period with the odds stacked against them? The answer is found in this chapter. Victory in Jesus is sure. He keeps everyone he seals. Hallelujah!

The Lamb and the 144,000 (14:1-5)

And I looked, and lo, a Lamb stood on the mount Sion, and with him an hundred forty and four thousand, having his Father's name written in their foreheads. And I heard a voice from heaven as the voice of many waters, and as the voice of great thunder: and I heard the voice of harpers harping with their harps: and they sung as it were a new song before the throne, and before the four beasts, and the elders: and no man could learn that song but the hundred and forty and four thousand, which were redeemed from the earth. These are they which were not defiled with women; for they are virgins. These are they which follow the Lamb whithersoever he goeth. These were redeemed from among men, being the firstfruits unto God and to the Lamb. And in their mouth was found no guile: for they are without fault before the throne of God (14:1-5).

New song of redemption (14:1-3)

The scene again "fast forwards" to the ultimate triumph of the Lamb at the beginning of the millennium on Mt. Zion in Jerusalem, where Christ will reign.

The Shepherd who began the Tribulation with 144,000 still has 144,000. He didn't lose one! He redeemed, sealed, and kept them. They came through the Tribulation like the three Hebrew boys came through the fiery furnace.

Not even Satan could separate them from God, and he can't separate you either, because you have been sealed by the Holy Spirit until the day of redemption if you have trusted Jesus Christ as your personal Savior.

Earth's rebellion will be over. Heaven and earth will be brought into wonderful harmony.

The "heavenly harpers" accompany the singers. These are not your typical church "angels," who are always up in the air harping about something. These harp on harps. Church angels, bless their harps, harp on just about everything but harps, unless there is a harp in the orchestra, in which case they harp on harps! Forgive me.

The 144,000 learn a new song that is exclusively theirs. It is redemption's song. Oh what a song they will sing, having experienced the mighty keeping power of God through hell on earth. Their accounts of narrow escapes will be fascinating to hear, no doubt. These are redeemed for the millennial earth by divine preservation, just as the Tribulation martyrs were redeemed through death.

Firstfruits for the kingdom (14:4-5)

The 144,000 are male virgin Jews – the Jehovah's Witnesses somehow missed that part. They are physical virgins, totally devoted to the Lamb and not to outside worries of families or immorality. They are also spiritual virgins who will not worship Satan or Antichrist. No group today can rightly claim to be the 144,000.

They are firstfruits, the cadre with which the Lamb will set up the millennial kingdom. "No guile" means "no deceit," as they won't fall for the lies of the beast. "Without fault" or blemish means they are clothed in the righteousness of Christ. Just as a new President of the United States has a cadre to set up his administration, the Lamb will use the 144,000 to establish his.

Four Proclamations (14:6-13)

John's vision in this interlude includes four proclamations. Let's take them one bite at a time.

Vision of the everlasting gospel (14:6-7)

And I saw another angel fly in the midst of heaven, having the everlasting gospel to preach unto them that dwell on the earth, and to every nation, and kindred, and tongue, and people, saying with a loud voice, Fear God, and give glory to him; for the hour of his judgment is come: and worship him that made heaven, and earth, and the sea, and the fountains of waters (14:6-7).

The gospel in our age is committed to men, not angels, but here the first of six angels preaches the "everlasting gospel." If the gospel is not communicated in the church age, it's our fault, not the angel's. But this is different. The church will be in Heaven, and the gospel preached by the angel is not the same gospel we preach.

The word gospel means "good news." This everlasting gospel is neither the gospel of grace nor of the kingdom, but the good news that God is about to deal with the world in righteousness and sovereignty. Fear (reverence) and worship are due him, because he is about to bring a heavy hammer down on sin and sinful people on earth. The Lion will roar! And when the Lion of the tribe of Judah roars, the jungle known as earth will tremble.

Vision of judgment on Babylon (14:8)

And there followed another angel, saying, Babylon is fallen, is fallen, that great city, because she made all nations drink of the wine of the wrath of her fornication (14:8).

Babylon is the place where idolatry began, and the city will apparently be rebuilt. It is my understanding that it is being rebuilt now. It was off limits to our troops that went into Iraq during Desert Storm.

The literal city will fall, religious Babylon will fall (Revelation 17), and commercial Babylon will fall (Revelation 18). Man's greatest enterprises and most serious attempts to displace God are all doomed. Prophetically, these are as corrupt as historic Babylon. How corrupt was historic Babylon? Glad you asked!

> *Babylon has been a golden cup in the Lord's hand, that made all the earth drunken: the nations have drunken of her wine; therefore the nations are mad (Jer 51:7).*

> *And Babylon, the glory of kingdoms, the beauty of the Chaldees' excellency, shall be as when God overthrew Sodom and Gomorrah (Isa 13:19).*

Babylon is considered by God in the same breath as Sodom and Gomorrah, and her judgment will be the same. In the Great Tribulation, Babylon represents absolute corruption and rebellion against God.

Vision of judgment on Beast worshippers (14:9-12)

> *And the third angel followed them, saying with a loud voice, If any man worship the beast and his image, and receive his mark in his forehead, or in his hand, the same shall drink of the wine of the wrath of God, which is poured out without mixture into the cup*

> *of his indignation; and he shall be tormented with fire and brimstone in the presence of the holy angels, and in the presence of the Lamb: and the smoke of their torment ascendeth up for ever and ever: and they have no rest day nor night, who worship the beast and his image, and whosoever receiveth the mark of his name. Here is the patience of the saints: here are they that keep the commandments of God, and the faith of Jesus (14:9-12).*

A neutral position will be impossible: no mark of the beast means starvation; receiving the mark means God's wrath and the lake of fire. Saints will love their families enough to watch them starve to death. Can you imagine the agony of mothers and fathers as their children cry for food day and night until they finally die? It breaks my heart when my grandchildren are hurt. I would do anything to ease their pain. In the Great Tribulation, parents and grandparents will face this choice: feed your children and grandchildren and lose them for eternity, or starve your children and preserve them for eternity.

Fire and brimstone were literal at Sodom and are literal here. If not, they are even worse. Eternity will be no party for those who die outside of Christ. Spiritual death is accompanied by physical, mental, and emotional anguish.

Consuming the wine of spiritual fornication causes drinking the wine of the wrath of God. There is no rest from torment "day nor night," "for ever and ever," no second chance to repent. Those who take the mark of the beast are eternally doomed and damned.

The lake of fire is apparently visible to Christ and the angels. Unbelief, unrepentance, and disobedience will be judged severely, The Tribulation saints patiently wait for the Lord's return in faith and obedience, though for most it will cost them their lives.

Vision of praise for those who die in the Lord (14:13)

And I heard a voice from heaven saying unto me, Write, Blessed are the dead which die in the Lord from henceforth: Yea, saith the Spirit, that they may rest from their labours; and their works do follow them (14:13).

The warning to beast worshippers is encouragement to those in Christ. In the Tribulation, it will be better to die at the hand of the beast than to live as a beast worshipper.

The Holy Spirit announces that death brings rest from sorrow and rewards for their faithful works. Death for saints will be precious – precious relief and precious relocation.

Preview of Armageddon (14:14-20)

John now sees a vision of Armageddon, that great battle which the Lord Jesus Christ will win with the Word of God from his mouth, and which we will study in some detail later.

Judgment of the Son of Man (14:14-16)

And I looked, and behold a white cloud, and upon the cloud one sat like unto the Son of man, having on his head a golden crown, and in his hand a sharp sickle. And another angel came out of the temple, crying with a loud voice to him that sat on the cloud, Thrust in thy sickle, and reap: for the time is come for thee to reap; for the harvest of the earth is ripe. And he that sat on the cloud thrust in his sickle on the earth; and the earth was reaped (14:14-16).

It's harvest time. A sickle is a sharp-bladed instrument used to harvest grain. The Lord himself comes on the shekinah cloud of glory to reap the harvest, according to his own description of the event in Matthew's Gospel.

> *Immediately after the tribulation of those days shall the sun be darkened, and the moon shall not give her light, and the stars shall fall from heaven, and the powers of the heavens shall be shaken: and then shall appear the sign of the Son of man in heaven: and then shall all the tribes of the earth mourn, and they shall see the Son of man coming in the clouds of heaven with power and great glory (Matt 24:29-30).*

He comes crowned as King, not Prophet or Priest. He wields the sickle of judgment in the earth where the angel says the harvest is "ripe," literally so ripe the fruit has begun to dry up and wither. Harvest is overdue.

> *Put ye in the sickle, for the harvest is ripe: come, get you down; for the press is full, the fats overflow, for their wickedness is great. Multitudes, multitudes in the valley of decision: for the day of the Lord is near in the valley of decision (Joel 3:13-14).*

The Megiddo plain or valley outside Jerusalem will be the valley of decision and the site of the most decisive military confrontation ever. The Lord himself swings his sickle of judgment and reaps the harvest.

Angel with the sharp sickle (14:17-20)

> *And another angel came out of the temple which is in heaven, he also having a sharp sickle. And*

another angel came out from the altar, which had power over fire; and cried with a loud cry to him that had the sharp sickle, saying, Thrust in thy sharp sickle, and gather the clusters of the vine of the earth; for her grapes are fully ripe. And the angel thrust in his sickle into the earth, and gathered the vine of the earth, and cast it into the great winepress of the wrath of God. And the winepress was trodden without the city, and blood came out of the winepress, even unto the horse bridles, by the space of a thousand and six hundred furlongs (14:17-20).

I don't think we can adequately imagine what this scene is like. The fifth angel comes from the temple in Heaven with a sharp sickle, indicating severe judgment. A sixth angel from the altar (in answer to the prayers of the martyrs in Revelation 6) exhorts the fifth to thrust in the sickle to grapes of wickedness, rebellion, and unrepentance that are overripe, as raisins.

As grapes are crushed to make wine, so the armies of the world will be crushed at Armageddon, and their blood will spurt from beneath the feet of the Judge. "Mine eyes have seen the glory of the coming of the Lord; He is trampling out the vintage where the grapes of wrath are stored."

The blood is said to be about four feet deep for 185 miles, the length of Palestine. The land is bathed with the blood of those who rejected the precious blood of Christ. It's his blood or their blood for their sin. It's his blood or yours for your sin.

If God is just, and he is, judgment will come. He will not tolerate sin on this earth any longer. He will not tolerate sin in your life, either. He's not coming again to die on a cross. He's coming again as absolute sovereign King of kings and Lord of lords. He came once as the Lamb of God;

he's coming again as the Lion of the tribe of Judah. And the world will tremble in shock and disbelief when this Lion roars, because they thought he was just a Lamb.

Sealed and Covered by the Blood

The church may experience suffering and tribulation, but the church will not go through the Great Tribulation. Most of the church has already missed that through death, and God's not going to resurrect them and send them back to go through it. That's the great fallacy in the argument that the church will go through the Tribulation. Is it all the church or just the part alive at the time? Will the body be divided?

The Great Tribulation is a terrible time, and it is miraculous that the 144,000 come through it. They'll make it, however, not because they are strong but because they are sealed and covered by the blood of the Lamb. So are you, if you are in Christ Jesus. And he'll never lose one of his own, not a single one.

Today is a day of grace, but God will ultimately judge all men. Today the invitation is still open to those who will, by faith, trust Jesus Christ as Savior and avail themselves of his grace, or unmerited favor. Today, by the grace of God, you can be sure you will not enter the awful Great Tribulation, which may well be pending for this present generation. Today is the day of salvation.

10
GOD'S WRATH
Revelation 15:1-8

Can a good and loving God ever get really mad? The Bible describes God as slow to anger, longsuffering, full of grace, and merciful. Could this same God be capable of extreme wrath?

Yes, he can get angry and yes, he is capable of extreme wrath.

This chapter is the preface to the final series of judgments upon the earth in the Great Tribulation, and they will be the most intense and devastating ever. The seventh seal included the seven trumpets, and the seventh trumpet included the seven vials or bowls of God's wrath introduced here. The purpose is judgment.

If you are trusting Jesus Christ, you will not go through the Great Tribulation. But you need to know what the unsaved will face. It will make you a better witness. If you understand the terrible plagues to come, and if you know your unsaved friends and relatives could be thrust into the Great Tribulation, you will warn them of the danger and encourage them to accept Christ. Failure to warn them of God's wrath would be irresponsible and uncaring.

Seven Angels With Seven Plagues (15:1)

And I saw another sign in heaven, great and marvellous, seven angels having the seven last plagues; for in them is filled up the wrath of God (15:1).

Another sign in heaven (15:1)

John had previously seen the signs of the woman, Israel, and the red dragon, Satan (Revelation 12:1, 3). This "great and marvelous" sign included seven angels with seven plagues, a burning sea of glass, and the temple of Heaven. The sign is called "great" because of its scope and intensity. It is described as "marvelous," causing wonder and amazement. *The Message* renders it "breathtaking."

Satan has been cast out of Heaven and has vented his wrath upon Israel. He has tried to dominate the world through his two beasts, Antichrist and the False Prophet.

The seven plagues will bring to an end God's judgment and signal the coming of Christ to earth. Like a brilliant diamond against a black felt background, Jesus will return in power and glory against the dark backdrop of the bowls of wrath. His return will be stunning, as we shall see.

The wrath of God (15:1)

The purpose of man is to glorify God. That makes God happy.

What makes God angry? What incurs his wrath? I have discovered six things in the Bible which really make God angry:

1. Idolatry (2 Chronicles 24:18).
2. Abusing his prophets (2 Chronicles 36:16).
3. Ungodliness and unrighteousness (Romans 1:18).

4. Unrepentance (Romans 2:5).
5. Worship of the beast (Revelation 14:10).
6. Not trusting Jesus Christ (John 3:36). The other five are, of course, related to this one. In that great third chapter of John, where we thrill to God's grace and love, we also find these words:

> *He that believeth on the Son hath everlasting life: and he that believeth not the Son shall not see life; but the wrath of God abideth on him.*

God's wrath is "filled up" in these seven last plagues. Those who don't glorify God must incur his complete wrath. The number seven speaks of completeness.

The Godly Victors (15:2-4)

As the stage continues to be set for the dispensing of the seven bowls of God's wrath, John's attention is drawn to some who gain the victory over the beast.

Their location and identification (15:2)

> *And I saw as it were a sea of glass mingled with fire: and them that had gotten the victory over the beast, and over his image, and over his mark, and over the number of his name, stand on the sea of glass, having the harps of God (15:2).*

John sees the sea of glass a second time (Revelation 4:6). Now, it appears to be mingled with fire. It is placid, representing God's rest; glassy, reflecting God's glory; stood upon, witness to God's faithfulness; and afire, witness to God's holy judgments. Who are the people standing on this sea of glass?

Their identification is given. They are the martyred dead who have gained the ultimate victory through faithfulness unto death. They did not worship the beast or his image, refused to take his mark or have any association with his number, and probably starved to death if they were not summarily executed. That may not sound like victory to us, but they traded the temporal for the eternal, and God calls that victory.

They are victorious, not bitter. They defied the beast, but didn't lose their song.

We need to be very careful to avoid bitterness in our lives, too. Bitterness can ruin a Christian's life. All of us know Christians who are bitter because of divorce, death of a family member, fraud in a business dealing, a perceived slight or wrong, illness, incapacitation, or any number of other things.

Bitterness is a poor witness, evidence of unforgiveness. We must guard against the root:

Looking diligently lest any man fail of the grace of God; lest any root of bitterness springing up trouble you, and thereby many be defiled (Heb 12:15).

We must not even let bitterness take root, because it defiles us and those around us.

Our "great tribulations" are small compared to those of the Tribulation saints. We need to look with faith beyond our present circumstances, confident that God will not only bring us through them, but that he also has something more wonderful and glorious awaiting us. Through eyes of faith, we see past our tears and suffering.

For his anger endureth but a moment; in his favour is life: weeping may endure for a night, but joy cometh in the morning (Ps 30:5).

> *For I reckon that the sufferings of this present time
> are not worthy to be compared with the glory which
> shall be revealed in us (Rom 8:18).*

We must not lose the joy of our salvation. The Great Tribulation martyrs kept things in proper perspective. They did not lose their joy – or their victory.

Their two songs (15:3-4)

> *And they sing the song of Moses the servant of God,
> and the song of the Lamb, saying, Great and
> marvellous are thy works, Lord God Almighty; just
> and true are thy ways, thou King of saints. Who shall
> not fear thee, O Lord, and glorify thy name? For thou
> only art holy: for all nations shall come and worship
> before thee; for thy judgments are made manifest
> (15:3-4).*

The song of Moses speaks of deliverance, salvation, and faithfulness (Exodus 15; Deuteronomy 32); the song of the Lamb ascribes praise to Christ as Redeemer (Revelation 5). The martyred throng sings both.

This is the "How Great Thou Art" of the martyrs. God is praised for his

     1. Tremendous and awe-inspiring works;
     2. Righteous and faithful ways;
     3. Sovereignty as ruler of saints/ages/nations;
     4. Right to fear and glory;
     5. Holiness;
     6. Universal worship;
     7. Reasonable, righteous, and revealed judgments.

In awesome wonder, the godly victors, who have been faithful through martyrdom, consider and recount the mighty works of God. What a song! What a Savior!

The Temple in Heaven (15:5-8)

The bowls of wrath will now be delivered to the selected angels who will pour them out upon the earth. The scene in Heaven is unbelievably solemn.

Priestly angels (15:5-6)

And after that I looked, and, behold, the temple of the tabenacle of the testimony in heaven was opened: and the seven angels came out of the temple, having the seven plagues, clothed in pure and white linen, and having their breasts girded with golden girdles (15:5-6).

The angels are dressed as Old Testament priests. We would understand by this that they are to perform a priestly service. Their departure from the temple signifies that they have already been purified for the task at hand.

There is a temple in Heaven (Revelation 11:19), after which the tabernacle on earth was patterned. God here deals with Israel, not the church, whose New Jerusalem home has no temple except for Christ and the Father (Revelation 21:22).

The "temple of the tabernacle of the testimony" is the Holy of holies, containing the ark of the covenant and the tables of stone. The ark's lid was both judgment seat and mercy seat. On the Day of Atonement, the high priest sprinkled blood on the lid of the ark of the covenant, and the sins of Israel were covered for the previous year. The judgment seat became the mercy seat. God was satisfied. Six times in the New Testament, Jesus is declared to be our mercy seat (propitiation, satisfaction). The shed blood of Jesus stands between the wrath of a holy and offended

God and wicked man. God the Father is satisfied with Christ's sacrifice. Are you? Have you by faith applied his blood to your life?

The seven angels appear as high priests departing the judgment seat to offer a great sacrifice to the offended holiness and justice of God.

Judgment will be by God's standard, the law, which was given to the Israelites to prove they could not attain God's requirements on their own. They thought they could. They told God they could. For 1,500 years they proved they could not. The blood sacrifice of the animals all those years pointed to the need for a perfect human sacrifice, and that was provided by the Lamb of God.

Without blood, there is judgment, but no mercy. The blood makes the judgment seat the mercy seat. Rejection of the blood means no mercy. Under the law it was the blood of animals that covered sin yearly:

> *For the law having a shadow of good things to come, and not the very image of the things, can never with those sacrifices which they offered year by year continually make the comers thereunto perfect. For then would they not have ceased to be offered? because that the worshippers once purged should have had no more conscience of sins. But in those sacrifices there is a remembrance again made of sins every year. For it is not possible that the blood of bulls and goats should take away sin (Heb 10:1-4).*

The blood of animals merely covered sin but made no one righteous through the removal of sin. Now it is the blood of Jesus that takes away sin forever –

> *By the which will we are sanctified through the offering of the body of Jesus Christ once for all. And*

every priest standeth daily ministering and offering oftentimes the same sacrifices, which can never take away sins: but this man, after he had offered one sacrifice for sins for ever, sat down on the right hand of God; from henceforth expecting till his enemies be made his footstool. For by one offering he hath perfected for ever them that are sanctified (Heb 10:10-14).

– and satisfies (propitiates) the Father:

But now the righteousness of God without the law is manifested, being witnessed by the law and the prophets; even the righteousness of God which is by faith of Jesus Christ unto all and upon all them that believe: for there is no difference: for all have sinned and come short of the glory of God; being justified freely by his grace through the redemption that is in Christ Jesus: whom God hath set forth to be a propitiation through faith in his blood, to declare his righteousness for the remission of sins that are past, through the forbearance of God (Rom 3:21-25).

The bowls of God's wrath (15:7)

And one of the four beasts gave unto the seven angels seven golden vials full of the wrath of God, who liveth for ever and ever (15:7).

One of the beasts, living creatures described in Revelation 4:6-8 as representing the attributes of Jesus Christ, gives the angels seven vials (bowls) full of the wrath of God, not his love.

The devastating character of this divine judgment is indicated by the word "full." It is complete, as indicated by seven angels and seven bowls. This judgment is unbelievably horrid, and cannot be released until God gives the command.

The glory of God (15:8)

And the temple was filled with smoke from the glory of God, and from his power; and no man was able to enter into the temple, till the seven plagues of the seven angels were fulfilled (15:8).

Isaiah was struck by God's glory and holiness in the temple filled with smoke (Isaiah 6:1-8). Here, Heaven's temple is filled with the smoke of God's glory and holiness till the bowls are poured out.

The bowls of God's wrath are to be poured out on a Christ-rejecting, blood-despising, and Hell-bound world. Christians of all ages will be vindicated; Great Tribulation martyrs will be avenged; Jesus Christ will be exalted; and God will be glorified –

Wherefore God also hath highly exalted him, and given him a name which is above every name: that at the name of Jesus every knee should bow, of things in heaven, and things in earth, and things under the earth; and that every tongue should confess that Jesus Christ is Lord, to the glory of God the Father (Phil 2:9-11).

God is unimaginably holy, holy, holy. The Son is to be exalted. That brings the Father glory. I have become so personally convicted of this truth that I make the first part of my early morning prayer something much like this: "Father, may you be glorified, may your Son be exalted, and may your Holy Spirit be obeyed in everything I think, do or say today." The Holy Spirit's mission is to exalt Jesus. Exaltation of Jesus glorifies the Father. How can I as a Christian not want to bring glory to my Father by exalting Jesus in obedience to the Holy Spirit?

What Will You Do with Jesus?

God's nature is unalterably opposed to sin. While he will take no pleasure in pouring out his wrath, he will be glorified because his Son will be exalted.

Remember this: Jesus Christ is the one being unveiled in Revelation. It is he who will direct the action during the Great Tribulation. It is the wrath of the Lamb that will startle the world. It is Jesus who is the Judge. It is his blood that determines Heaven or Hell for you. It is his wrath that is upon you if you reject him. It is he to whom you will answer.

What is your answer? What will you do with Jesus?

What will you do about your unsaved friends and relatives? Will you warn them of judgment to come? Will you tell them that Jesus died for them? Or will you let them fend for themselves and perhaps die under the wrath of God? Will you be a witness?

11

THE SEVEN BOWLS OF GOD'S WRATH

Revelation 16:1-21

I fail to see how anyone could spiritualize the seven bowls of God's wrath. A lady told me recently she did not believe what I said about the Book of Revelation. Her entire denomination, she said, "ignored" this prophecy. Why would God promise a blessing to those who read and hear the Revelation (Revelation 1:3) if it was not meant to be read or understood? He wouldn't.

God wanted us to know what will happen. The scenario is one even Stephen King could not imagine.

Others claim the plagues are symbolic, not literal. If that is true, get ready for some symbolic sores, blood, heat, darkness, frogs, and earthquakes, because they are all here. I wonder what a symbolic frog looks and sounds like! Does he croak "Bud-weis-er"?

World events now rush to the climatic return of our Lord Jesus Christ in power and glory. In rapid succession and with increasing intensity, the seven vials or bowls of

God's direct judgment are poured out on the entire world. Christ is still in charge, and he commands the angels to execute God's wrath upon a Christ-rejecting world.

Nothing this awful has ever happened on the earth. God hates sin, and his wrath now overflows in judgment.

The First Six Bowls (16:1-12)

The first six bowls are poured out in rapid succession, followed by a parenthesis. Then the seventh dreadful bowl is spilled upon the earth just preceding the return of Christ in power and glory.

The command is given (16:1)

And I heard a great voice out of the temple saying to the seven angels, Go your ways, and pour out the vials of the wrath of God upon the earth (16:1).

The hour arrives, God himself gives the command, and the angels move with military precision to carry out their marching orders. Previous judgments were sometimes restricted to one-third of earth or men; these are universal.

Saints have suffered and died by not being able to buy or sell. Now God's great voice thunders great judgment upon great sinners and the earth. The bowls of God's mercy and grace now overflow with his wrath and judgment. The offended party judges the unrepentant.

Six plagues are poured out (16:2-12)

Here the final plagues come in rapid order. It's bang, bang, bang! There's no time to recover from one before another hits.

First bowl: sores on Satan's men (16:2)

And the first went, and poured out his vial upon the earth; and there fell a noisome and grievous sore upon the men which had the mark of the beast, and upon them which worshipped his image (6:2)

These putrifying and incurable boils, worse than cancer or leprosy, reveal physically what those with the mark of the beast are morally — utterly corrupt. God sees the insides of these unrepentant and unbelieving sinners as pus-filled pockets of repugnant rebellion. They chose the Antichrist over the Christ, so God reveals on the outside for what they are on the inside.

Second bowl: the sea becomes blood (16:3)

And the second angel poured out his vial upon the sea; and it became as the blood of a dead man; and every living soul died in the sea (16:3).

The total sea becomes as the blood of a dead man, a stinking grave of death for every soul in the sea. The sea, which covers three-fourths of the earth's surface, is teeming with life. Every living thing in the sea dies. Every whale, shark, dolphin, oyster, shrimp, red snapper, flounder, and blue marlin dies.

Think of the stench as these dead creatures first float to the top and then wash ashore around the world. The water of the sea will no longer sustain life, having become blood like that of a dead man. It is oxygen-depleted. Even the coral dies. The sea becomes one huge graveyard.

Those who didn't cancel their vacation trips to the beach after the second trumpet will certainly change their plans after the second bowl!

Third bowl: fresh water becomes blood (16:4-7)

And the third angel poured out his vial upon the rivers and fountains of waters; and they became blood. And I heard the angel of the waters say, Thou art righteous, O Lord, which art, and wast, and shalt be, because thou hast judged thus. For they have shed the blood of saints and prophets, and thou hast given them blood to drink; for they are worthy. And I heard another out of the altar say, Even so, Lord God Almighty, true and righteous are thy judgments (16:4-7).

The world's total water supply becomes blood. The "angel of the waters" declares this is poetic justice — those who spill blood drink blood. "Let 'em drink blood!" he says. They were bloodthirsty in their murders of the saints and prophets, so they will now satisfy their thirst with literal blood.

The trout, catfish, and bass now join their saltwater cousins in bloody graves – and the smell gets worse!

Fourth bowl: the sun's heat increases (16:8-9)

And the fourth angel poured out his vial upon the sun; and power was given unto him to scorch men with fire. And men were scorched with great heat, and blasphemed God, which hath power over these plagues: and they repented not to give him glory (16:8-9).

The balance of nature is now upset, and global warming becomes a reality. Temperatures rise dramatically, and Satan's men are scorched. Do they repent? Do they recognize that God, not Satan, is in charge? Do they bow down before the Christ instead of the Antichrist? No. They blaspheme God rather than repent. The human heart is incurably wicked, and no amount of punishment will purify or change it. Apart from the work of the Holy Spirit, the human heart will never turn to God. By the way, the heat intensifies the disgusting stench of dead creatures, blood, and putrifying boils.

Fifth bowl: darkness and pain (16:10-11)

And the fifth angel poured out his vial upon the seat of the beast; and his kingdom was full of darkness; and they gnawed their tongues for pain, and blasphemed the God of heaven, because of their pains and their sores, and repented not of their deeds (16:10-11).

Their sores get sorer. Tongues are gnawed in agony. The result is blasphemy, not repentance.

Men in Hell will not repent, either. They will acknowledge Jesus as Lord, but they will never repent.

Isaiah, Joel, Nahum, Amos, Zephaniah, and Christ all predicted this coming darkness.

Sixth bowl: Euphrates River dries up (16:12)

And the sixth angel poured out his vial upon the great river Euphrates; and the water thereof was dried up, that the way of the kings of the East might be prepared (16:12).

The cradle of civilization, eastern border of the Promised Land and the Roman Empire, 1800 miles long, supernaturally dries up to allow the kings of the sunrising a clear approach to Armageddon. An army of 200 million will come from the east (rising sun). To cross the Euphrates River would be difficult, though not impossible. God dries up the river to facillitate their advance. Nothing can be allowed to delay the coming of the Lord at Armageddon. Everything and everybody must be in place.

Vision of Armageddon (16:13-16)

The first six bowls are terrible. The seventh is worse. But first we need to catch our breath with this parenthetical pause.

The unclean spirits (16:13-14)

And I saw three unclean spirits like frogs come out of the mouth of the dragon, and out of the mouth of the beast, and out of the mouth of the false prophet. For they are the spirits of devils, working miracles, which go forth unto the kings of the earth, and of the whole world, to gather them to the battle of that great day of God Almighty (16:13-14).

The unholy trinity of Hell – Satan, Antichrist, and False Prophet – brainwash the nations of the world into marching against Israel.

The unclean spirits that come out of the mouths of the unholy trinity are like frogs. In Egypt the frogs were literal. One of the most humorous accounts in the Bible occurs during the contest between Moses and Pharaoh, when Pharaoh requests one more night with the frogs (Exodus 8:6-11). The frog-like spirits in our text are demonic, miracle-working, and influential.

The gathering is to destroy God's purposes on earth and his covenants with Israel. Satan is unalterably opposed to Israel, the woman who produced the child, Christ. He hates what Israel is yet to become. God promised Abraham the land, David the kingdom. Israel has never occupied all the land promised to Abraham, but she will. God promised David the kingdom forever, which will be realized in his son, Jesus Christ.

Through the unclean spirits, Satan brainwashes the kings of the earth into sending their armies to Israel. They come for a bloodbath. Let's check with Brother Daniel:

> *And the king shall do according to his will; and he shall exalt himself, and magnify himself above every god, and shall speak marvellous things against the God of gods, and shall prosper till the indignation be accomplished: for that that is determined shall be done. Neither shall he regard the God of his fathers, nor the desire of women, nor regard any god: for he shall magnify himself above all. But in his estate shall he honour the God of forces: and a god whom his fathers knew not shall he honour with gold, and silver, and with precious stones, and pleasant things. Thus shall he do in the most strong holds with a strange god, whom he shall acknowledge and increase with glory: and he shall cause them to rule over many, and shall divide the land for gain (Dan 11:36-39).*

Antichrist exalts himself and worships the Devil. He may be homosexual, disregarding "the desire of women." He understands and uses military force. The God and traditions of his ancestors mean nothing to him. His god is Satan, and his only tradition is himself. He is a "legend in his own mind." His irrationality is evidence of demon possession and demon control. I am convinced he is Satan incarnate.

And at the time of the end shall the king of the south push at him: and the king of the north shall come against him like a whirlwird, with chariots, and with horsemen, and with many ships; and he shall enter into the countries, and shall overflow and pass over. He shall enter also into the glorious land, and many countries shall be overthrown: but these shall escape out of his hand, even Edom, and Moab, and the chief of the children of Ammon. He shall stretch forth his hand also upon the countries: and the land of Egypt shall not escape. But he shall have power over the treasures of gold and of silver, and over all the precious things of Egypt: and the Libyans and the Ethiopians shall be at his steps. But tidings out of the east and out of the north shall trouble him: therefore he shall go forth with great fury to destroy, and utterly to make away many. And he shall plant the tabernacles of his palace between the seas in the glorious holy mountain; yet he shall come to his end, and none shall help him (Dan 11:40-45).

Antichrist is intelligent. He doesn't care why the armies of the world come to Israel, as long as they do. Some come to fight with him, some against him. Pressure from the north and south and news from the east of the approaching 200 million man army get his attention.

It has apparently dawned on some that the cause of the plagues is Antichrist. They come to engage him in battle. Others still support him. No matter. He figures if he can get them there, they will join him in a fight against the soon-coming Lord Jesus Christ.

Russia is not finished. She is the army from the north. The African nations from the south and the nations from the Orient all come for the greatest bloodbath ever. They do not know that the blood will be their own.

The thief (16:15)

> *Behold, I come as a thief. Blessed is he that watcheth, and keepeth his garments, lest he walk naked, and they see his shame (16:15).*

A thief is someone who is not welcome, someone to be shut out, someone who causes loss. I don't want a thief in my house. A thief violates someone else's space and property.

Christ will never come as a thief to the church, because the church is not in darkness.

> *But ye, brethren, are not in darkness, that that day should overtake you as a thief (1 Thess 5:4).*

But he will come as a thief at the end of the Great Tribulation — not welcome, shut out, causing loss.

Those watching and clothed in the righteousness of Christ are "blessed." A guard found asleep on his watch in John's day was either beaten or had his garments set on fire. That'll make an impression!

If the Viet Cong discovered two American soldiers asleep in the same foxhole, they would often kill just one of them. Can you imagine how hard it was for the one left alive to sleep again?

When I returned from Vietnam, I was charged with training Infantry soldiers for duty in Vietnam. When I found both men asleep in the same foxhole, I dropped a smoke grenade – sometimes a tear gas grenade – into the foxhole. When they awakened in panic, they did seek to escape! Some ran through the woods screaming. Lesson taught and learned – be alert! Lives saved in Vietnam.

The world will not be looking for Jesus at Armageddon, but he will know right where to find them.

The gathering (16:16)

And he gathered them together into a place called in the Hebrew tongue, Armageddon (16:16).

Armageddon, "Mount of Slaughter" or "Mount of Megiddo," is adjacent to the plain of Megiddo to the west and the plain of Esdraelon to the northeast and the site of many past battles. Napoleon said, "What an excellent place into which all the armies of the world could be maneuvered." How prophetic.

This will be the focal point for a war that will cover an area some 200 miles north to south. It's not just a battle, but a continuing campaign, a war.

The armies of the world march against Israel and Antichrist but will turn against Christ himself. How futile.

The Seventh Bowl (16:17-21)

The seventh bowl is the most horrible and immediately precedes the second coming of Christ in power and glory. If he did not return at this time, everybody on earth would die, with the exception of those divinely preserved.

The announcement (16:17-18)

And the seventh angel poured out his vial into the air; and there came a great voice out of the temple of heaven, from the throne, saying, It is done. And there were voices, and thunders, and lightnings; and there was a great earthquake, such as was not since men were upon the earth, so mighty an earthquake, and so great (16:17-18).

This bowl of wrath is poured out in the atmosphere and is introduced by voices, thunders, and lightnings from heaven. All of nature is now under judgment.

A great voice, probably of the Son of God, announces, "It is done." On the cross he said, "It is finished." On the cross, redemption was paid, so Christ reported, "It is finished," or "paid in full." This judgment is the final act preceeding the second coming of Christ, so he reports, "It is done."

The greatest earthquake ever shakes the world. The whole world literally convulses. It is as if the Creator takes the earth in his hands and gives it a good shaking. Let's see what happens.

Earthquake and hail (16:19-21)

And the great city was divided into three parts, and the cities of the nations fell: and great Babylon came in remembrance before God, to give unto her the cup of the wine of the fierceness of his wrath. And every island fled away, and the mountains were not found. And there fell upon men a great hail out of heaven, every stone about the weight of a talent: and men blasphemed God because of the plague of the hail; for the plague thereof was exceeding great (16:19-21).

Spiritualize this if you can. I cannot.

The earthquake changes the world's topography. All the cities fall. Jerusalem (or Babylon or Rome?) is divided into three parts. Every island shifts from one place to another. Every mountain in the world is leveled. The Richter Scale has not been made that can measure this earthquake. What does God mean if he does not mean a great earthquake which will make the world convulse?

Great hailstones bombard the earth. A Greek talent weighs 56 pounds, a Jewish talent 114 pounds. These are not your run-of-the-mill dime-sized or tennis ball-sized hailstones! These kill anybody they strike – instantly.

This judgment is greater in destruction than Sodom and Gomorrah, and this one covers the entire earth.

Do men repent? No, they blaspheme God! Amazing.

Perverse and Without Excuse

Paul wrote that men who witness the power of God in creation are without excuse and guilty before God. The world in the Great Tribulation will see God's mighty hand revealed in judgment, but men will blaspheme rather than repent.

The utter perversity of human nature, which will reject the sovereign God in the face of such overwhelming evidence, confirms that even in the lake of fire men will not repent. How perverse! How depraved man is outside Christ. Those who harden their hearts against the grace of God will not escape divine judgment.

Many have hardened their hearts against him in this age. Now he offers salvation to all who believe, but his patience will soon end, and he will pour out his vengeance on a Christ-rejecting world.

Is Jesus your Savior, or will he be your Judge?

12

THE GREAT HARLOT

Revelation 17:1-18

On March 6, 1990, my mother cut off all communication with me because, in her words, I was a member of the "harlot church." Is it possible that she was right? Who is the great whore or prostitute of Revelation 17, and what is the harlot church?

In this chapter we deal with ecclesiastical Babylon, in the next with commercial Babylon. The word "ecclesiastical" is a favorite among preachers because it has a lot of syllables; therefore it sounds impressive and confuses the laity (those not in the ministry). The word speaks of the church or "called out assembly," so we know it has something to do with religion.

Ecclesiastical Babylon is the apostate church that remains after the true church is raptured. It will be tolerated by the beast, hated by the beast, and destroyed by the beast at the mid-point of the Great Tribulation. Commercial Babylon, on the other hand, will be loved by the beast and the world but destroyed by the return of Christ at the end of the Great Tribulation Period.

By the way, I am not in the "harlot church." In this case, at least, mother does not know best.

The Harlot Rides the Beast (17:1-7)

As we saw in the last chapter, the seventh bowl of God's wrath immediately precedes the second coming of Christ in power and glory. Revelation 17 does not come after the seventh bowl, but is an overview of the unbelieving church and its relation to Antichrist during the Tribulation.

She's an adulteress (17:1-2)

And there came one of the seven angels which had the seven vials, and talked with me, saying unto me, Come hither; I will shew unto thee the judgment of the great whore that sitteth upon many waters: with whom the kings of the earth have committed fornication, and the inhabitants of the earth have been made drunk with the wine of her fornication (17:1-2).

This woman is a great whore that sits upon or controls masses of people. Outwardly, she has the name of the true God but serves other gods. She is unfaithful to the name she carries. That is spiritual adultery, as surely as infidelity in a marriage is physical adultery.

The true church will be gone. Actually, the religious crowd that remains will be more guilty of fornication than adultery, because they will never have been married to the Christ whose name they claim. They "assume" the name of Christ without bothering to get married to him.

The kings of the world love and embrace her. Church and state are allied worldwide. Politicians throughout history who have been able to claim the support of the church have wielded great power.

All religions are united ecumenically for the first time. This false religion and moral wickedness cause a spiritual stupefying drunkenness throughout the world. Everything must be all right with the world, because religion and politics have finally come together. Such thinking will prevail for the first half of the Tribulation.

She's a prostitute (17:3-5)

So he carried me away in the spirit into the wilderness: and I saw a woman sit upon a scarlet coloured beast, full of names of blasphemy, having seven heads and ten horns. And the woman was arrayed in purple and scarlet colour, and decked with gold and precious stones and pearls, having a golden cup in her hand full of abominations and filthiness of her fornication: and upon her forehead was a name written, MYSTERY, BABYLON THE GREAT, THE MOTHER OF HARLOTS AND ABOMINATIONS OF THE EARTH (17:3-5).

The beast is the Antichrist and his restored Roman Empire. His description in the third verse leaves no doubt as to his identity.

The woman is religious Rome. She rides (controls) the beast. Her array is the purple of Roman imperialism, the scarlet of Roman Catholicism, and the gold of deity. She's the one-world religious system. This is not to be misinterpreted as Catholic bashing, but rather a recognition that the seat of this false church in the Great Tribulation is Rome.

At the same time, we must admit that many of the rituals and trappings of Romanism can be traced to

Babylonian paganism. Roman papacy has dominated many political states. A politician with the Roman church in his corner will have great power. We must not compromise in the name of religious unity or for the sake of political favoritism.

The woman's intoxicant is spiritual fornication. She gets high on her role as a dominatrix to the most powerful man in the world. She prostitutes herself to be beast for the status and power she is granted. The mark of her profession is in her forehead:

1. "Mystery" — something not previously revealed.
2. "Babylon the Great" — Babylon has always meant rebellion, human pride, and idolatry.
3. "Mother of harlots" — antithesis of the true church, the virgin bride of Christ. What a name!
4. Mother of "abominations" — she is evil.

She's a drunk (17:6-7)

And I saw the woman drunken with the blood of the saints, and with the blood of the martyrs of Jesus: and when I saw her, I wondered with great admiration. And the angel said unto me, Wherefore didst thou marvel? I will tell thee the mystery of the woman, and of the beast that carrieth her, which hath the seven heads and ten horns (17:6-7).

Apostate Christendom has always persecuted true believers. During the Inquisition, hundreds of thousands of true believers were killed in the name of religion by the established church of the day.

This whore not only makes others drunk, but she is intoxicated by her own acts of persecution. She cannot get enough. The more blood she sees, the more she wants. She becomes a bloodaholic, an addict.

John is amazed to see organized religion (cults, Romanism, and Protestantism) so corrupted. He cannot believe his eyes! The angel promises to explain the mystery and immediately proceeds to do so.

The Beast the Harlot Rides (17:8-14)

You are about to learn my secret. You may have thought I was winging it in my interpretation of the first seven verses. Actually, I had already read the last 11 verses and used what the angel said. "Johnny," he said (They were real close by this time!), "let me explain what you just saw." He started with the beast.

His origin (17:8-11)

The beast that thou sawest was, and is not; and shall ascend out of the bottomless pit, and go into perdition: and they that dwell on the earth shall wonder, whose names were not written in the book of life from the foundation of the world, when they behold the beast that was, and is not, and yet is (17:8).

This does require a little explanation, doesn't it?

And here is the mind which hath wisdom. The seven heads are seven mountains, on which the woman sitteth. And there are seven kings: five are fallen, and one is, and the other is not yet come; and when he cometh, he must continue a short space. And the beast that was, and is not, even he is the eighth, and is of the seven, and goeth into perdition (17:9-11).

That really cleared things up, didn't it?

The beast is Antichrist and his empire, empowered by Satan himself. It is the Roman empire ("that was"), seemingly dead ("and is not"), that has been revived ("and yet is"). It will be destroyed when Christ returns. Not just the system, but the man himself is in view here. In his imitation of Christ, the beast will suffer a supposedly fatal wound and be resurrected.

Here is another area of great disagreement. The seven mountains seem to be Rome, which will be ecclesiastical Babylon, home to the world church. Some see them as the seven great empires which have enjoyed or will enjoy world power (Egypt, Assyria, Babylon, Persia, Greece, Rome, and revived Rome). All loved the whore and utilized the combination of church and state, or religion and politics, to great advantage.

The seven kings have been interpreted as six previous Roman emperors and one to come, as well as seven forms of Roman government.   Seven also speaks of completeness. Regardless, the reactivated Roman Empire is in view. The beast comes from that setting. His earthly origin is probably Europe, his spiritual origin "the bottomless pit," and his destination "perdition."

His kingdom (17:12-14)

And the ten horns which thou sawest are ten kings, which have received no kingdom as yet; but receive power as kings one hour with the beast. These have one mind, and shall give their power and strength unto the beast. These shall make war with the Lamb, and the Lamb shall overcome them: for he is Lord of lords, and King of kings: and they that are with him are called, and chosen, and faithful (17:12-14).

A ten-nation confederacy has three of its members overcome by one who takes over, becoming eighth (10 - 3 + 1 = 8). All the others give him power and support because he has three marbles, and each of them only has one marble. That's the way Antichrist comes to power. The one with the most marbles names the game, and everybody else either agrees or takes his marble and goes home. In the Tribulation, the kings (or presidents or prime ministers) all decide they want to play marbles with the Antichrist, so they pledge themselves – and their countries – to him, because he has he most marbles.

They not only persecute true believers (called, chosen, and faithful – praise the Lord!) but also make war with the Lamb — what a mistake! Even one who controls ten marbles will never be as powerful as the King of kings and Lord of lords, because he is omnipotent, and all the marbles belong to him.

The beast that the harlot rides is Antichrist.

The Beast Destroys the Harlot (17:15-18)

There comes a time in the life of every prostitute when she is no longer needed by her lover. When that time comes, she is discarded.

The waters where the whore sits (17:15)

And he saith unto me, The waters which thou sawest, where the whore sitteth, are peoples, and multitudes, and nations, and tongues (17:15).

The waters sat upon or covered by the woman are vast numbers of peoples, multitudes, nations, and tongues. The angel gives us the interpretation. The harlot has tremendous influence for a period of time.

During the first half of the Tribulation, the woman controls the people of the world and shares power with the beast, to whom she is useful. As long as she can provide him the loyalty of the combined religious community of the world, he keeps her around, and she rides him for all he is worth.

The death the whore suffers (17:16-18)

And the ten horns which thou sawest upon the beast, these shall hate the whore, and shall make her desolate, and naked, and shall eat her flesh, and burn her with fire. For God hath put in their hearts to fulfil his will, and to agree, and give their kingdom unto the beast, until the words of God shall be fulfilled. And the woman which thou sawest is that great city, which reigneth over the kings of the earth (17:16-18).

The beast may tolerate the harlot, but he hates her. Not only will he break his covenant with Israel, but he will also cannibalistically destroy this false church when it is of no further use to him. He is not one to share power for long, because he covets all power and worship.

The false church should not be surprised at this turn of events. She has lived a life of unfaithfulness, and now the tables are turned. It is always amazing to me that those who have affairs, divorce their spouses, and marry their affair partners are so shocked when their new spouses have affairs with someone else. It's very common. Those who engage in adultery need not be surprised when their partners in unfaithfulness become unfaithful. A prostitute or adulteress is usually discarded when she is of no further benefit.

By eliminating the apostate church, the way is cleared for worship of Antichrist as promoted and demanded by the False Prophet. Antichrist must destroy the false church so the False Prophet can declare him "Christ" and demand that everyone worship him. The competition must be eliminated.

The unholy trinity claims for itself all religious, political, and commercial power. That's as much power as any human can have. Even this fulfills God's purpose and plan.

The woman is identified by her headquarters, Rome, and she has great dominion for awhile. But she's a whore, a prostitute, and she is eventually discarded.

The Bride Is Not a Harlot

The challenge for us today is to remain pure in doctrine and the fundamentals of the faith. We must not compromise, though the cry for ecumenical unity and a one-world church will steadily increase until it becomes a reality in the Great Tribulation. As we have seen, that movement is doomed to failure at the hands of the beast, who will himself be defeated by the King of kings and Lord of lords, Jesus Christ.

We are the bride of Christ, not the harlot church. Let's remain faithful. Let's remember to whom we will answer. It's not what people think that ultimately matters.

There's one more issue: If you are not in Christ, you are just as guilty and deserving of Hell as any apostate. If you die without Christ, you will share eternity with the Antichrist, the apostates, the deviants, the perverts, and the unbelievers of all ages, because you truly are one of them. Won't you identify yourself as one of the called, the chosen, and the faithful by trusting Jesus Christ as your Savior today? He will win, and you can only win through him.

13

THE FALL OF BABYLON

Revelation 18:1-24

Every time Alan Greenspan sneezes, Wall Street catches a cold. Greenspan, chairman of the Federal Reserve Board, can suggest an interest rate hike or question investor optimism, and the market will react.

When the stock market crashed in 1929, the United States plunged into the Great Depression. Inflation soared, many lost their entire fortunes, and a significant number committed suicide. When the stock market tumbled in 1987, many were ruined financially.

Imagine what would happen if the New York Stock Exchange, the London Exchange, the Tokyo Exchange, and all the other major markets in the world were combined into one, and that one were to not only crash but also go completely out of existence in one day. That's exactly what the Bible says will happen just before Christ returns in power and glory. The Babylon Exchange, through which Antichrist will control the commercial world, will go "belly up" in a single hour of God's judgment. Things will change in an instant. Antichrist will be out of "business" in one hour.

On a recent Sunday morning, I arose from bed and headed for the bathroom. I remember feeling dizzy and reaching for the door jamb to steady myself. I missed and awoke lying on the bathroom floor, my nose broken and bleeding. Here is wisdom: If you are going to pick a fight with a tile floor, don't lead with your face! Also, if you are going to defy an opponent, don't let that opponent be the omnipotent King of kings and Lord of lords. In both cases, you will lose, as the commercial world will discover in the Great Tribulation.

Babylon's Fall Announced (18:1-8)

Another Babylon is now introduced. Whereas Mystery Babylon, the apostate church, was tolerated but hated by Antichrist and the kings of the earth, commercial Babylon is embraced and loved. Think it has anything to do with money?

The announcement (18:1-3)

And after these things I saw another angel come down from heaven, having great power; and the earth was lightened with his glory. And he cried mightily with a loud voice, saying, Babylon the great is fallen, is fallen, and is become the habitation of devils, and the hold of every foul spirit, and a cage of every unclean and hateful bird. For all nations have drunk of the wine of the wrath of her fornication, and the kings of the earth have committed fornication with her, and the merchants of the earth are waxed rich through the abundance of her delicacies (18:1-3).

This Babylon is economic, loved by the kings of the earth. Mystery Babylon was the apostate church, hated and finally destroyed by earth's kings in the middle of the Great Tribulation to pave the way for worship of Antichrist. Mystery Babylon is Rome; commercial Babylon is probably ancient Babylon rebuilt or any center of world trade determined by Antichrist. New York would be a natural choice.

"After these things" — The destruction of commercial Babylon happens after the harlot expires. The harlot is destroyed midpoint in the Tribulation. Commercial Babylon's fall happens later, at Tribulation's very end, just before Jesus returns in power and glory.

"Another angel" (same kind as Revelation 17:1) is not Christ but has great authority, power, and prestige. His announcement is in the Greek prophetic aorist tense, which means it is sure of happening at a point in time.

When Babylon falls it becomes the habitat or cage of demons, unclean spirits, and unclean birds for the duration of the millennium. Babylon always symbolizes rebellion and demonic activity. The Tower of Babel was Nimrod's attempt to unite the world's religions under an astrological umbrella in rebellion against God.

This is God's announced judgment on the brokers of big business for big profit who had no time for God. Those in the market have become filthy rich, and the leaders of the nations have padded their pockets, too. The kings are said to have committed fornication with the market. Their greed has obliterated their loyalty to their nations.

The separation (18:4-5)

And I heard another voice from heaven, saying, Come out of her, my people, that ye be not partakers of her sins, and that ye receive not of her plagues.

*For her sins have reached unto heaven, and God hath
remembered her iniquities (18:4-5).*

Another voice, probably Christ's, calls God's own out
of Babylon as Lot was called from Sodom:
    1. So as not to partake of Babylon's sins.
    2. To avoid the judgment upon Babylon.
This may well be the resurrection of Old Testament and
Tribulation saints in conjunction with the return of Christ.

God has the record of Babylon's sins, and his
judgment, though delayed, is nevertheless sure. Just
because God doesn't judge sin when we think he should
doesn't mean he is not going to judge sin. He will.

God calls us to be separate, too, and to judge our own
sin by confessing and forsaking:

*For if we would judge ourselves, we should not be
judged. But when we are judged, we are chastened of
the Lord, that we should not be condemned with the
world (1 Cor 11:31-32).*

*If we confess our sins, he is faithful and just to forgive
us our sins, and to cleanse us from all
unrighteousness (1 John 1:9).*

We judge ourselves by confession (*homologeo* – say the
same word, or agree with God that our sin is sin). When
we confess, God wipes the slate clean. Too easy? Take it
up with God. He made the rules.

The sentence (18:6-8)

*Reward her even as she rewarded you, and double
unto her double according to her works: in the cup
which she hath filled fill to her double. How much*

> *she hath glorified herself, and lived deliciously, so much torment and sorrow give her: for she saith in her heart, I sit a queen, and am no widow, and shall see no sorrow. Therefore, shall her plagues come in one day, death, and mourning, and famine; and she shall be utterly burned with fire: for strong is the Lord God who judgeth her (18:6-8)*

Normal judgment is "eye for eye," but Babylon's apostasy is so enormous, her lifestyle so wanton, her arrogance so repugnant, that she is to be judged double double and without mercy. She lived "deliciously." What an interesting description. She wanted nothing because she had all the luxuries and delicacies imaginable. She proclaimed her own importance and invincibility. "Lay it on thick!" Jesus commands.

The handwriting is again on the wall for Babylon (Daniel 5), and her destruction is total, final, and accomplished by God in a single hour. Commercial Babylon will be weighed in the balances and found wanting, just as Belshazzar's Babylon was.

Babylon's Fall Mourned (18:9-19)

Not everyone is going to stand up and cheer when Babylon bites the dust. The wail that goes up is pitiful and laughable at the same time. Ask yourself this question: Would it break my heart if the stock market crashed today? If your whole life revolves around making money, your answer may be yes. Would you cry in despair?

The kings of the earth mourn (18:9-10)

> *And the kings of the earth, who have committed fornication and lived deliciously with her, shall*

bewail her, and lament for her, when they shall see the smoke of her burning. Standing afar off, for the fear of her torment, saying, Alas, alas, that great city, Babylon, that mighty city! For in one hour is thy judgment come (18:9-10).

Babylon will be the headquarters of Antichrist, the world center of political and commercial power. By day's end, she is nothing but smoldering ruins.

The kings who participated in her wickedness and wealth mourn her passing in a contemptible and pathetic manner. They loved her and loved their rewarding adulterous relationship with her. They have sold their souls for money, and now their precious money is gone.

They marvel from afar at the market's sudden destruction. Isn't that human nature? When a person starts having severe financial problems, so-called friends often "marvel from afar" rather than lend a hand or a buck!

The merchants of the earth mourn (18:11-19)

And the merchants of the earth shall weep and mourn over her; for no man buyeth their merchandise any more: the merchandise of gold, and silver, and precious stones, and of pearls, and fine linen, and purple, and silk, and scarlet, and all thyine wood, and all manner vessels of ivory, and all manner vessels of most precious wood, and of brass, and iron, and marble, and cinnamon, and odours, and ointments, and frankincense, and wine, and oil, and fine flour, and wheat, and beasts, and sheep, and horses, and chariots, and slaves, and souls of men (18:11-13).

Are you paying attention? They sell everything, including people. Anything for money.

And the fruits that thy soul lusteth after are departed from thee, and all things which were dainty and goodly are departed from thee, and thou shalt find them no more at all.

The merchants of these things, which were made rich by her, shall stand afar off for the fear of her torment, weeping and wailing, and saying, Alas, alas, that great city, that was clothed in fine linen, and purple, and scarlet, and decked with gold, and precious stones, and pearls! For in one hour so great riches is come to nought (18:14-17a).

The merchants send up a wail (*ouai, ouai!*) for their loss of trade and source of income. The sound of their lament is "Why, why?" "Alas, alas," their lifestyles have come crashing down around them.

The 28 items mentioned are luxuries: jewelry, fine furnishings, spices and cosmetics, liquors, and pastries, the best cuts of meat, fine cars, even men and their souls. They had completely abandoned themselves to the wealth of the world.

Suddenly, in an hour, it is all gone. The stock market and commodities market have crashed. The merchants have no merchandise and no money.

The captains of the sea mourn (18:17b-19)

And every shipmaster, and all the company in ships, and sailors, and as many as trade by sea, stood afar off, and cried when they saw the smoke of her burning, saying, What city is like unto this great city! And they cast dust on their heads, and cried, weeping and wailing, saying, Alas, alas that great city, wherein were made rich all that had ships in the sea by reason of her costliness! For in one hour is she made desolate (18:17b-19).

The shipmasters cry and weep because of the sudden depression. Not only have they had to plot their courses through seas that have turned to stinking blood and floating dead fish, under a sun that is hotter than ever and yet in increased darkness, and with no islands or mountains to naviagate by, but now there is no market for their goods. All their investments are worthless in a flash.

Babylon's religious, political, and economic rule of the world is gone. All is chaos.

Would it break your heart if the world's economic system collapsed? Where's your treasure, here or in Heaven? Your answer will tell you where your heart really is, according to Jesus.

Lay not up for yourselves treasures upon earth, where moth, and rust doth corrupt, and where thieves break through and steal: but lay up for yourselves treasures in heaven, where neither moth nor rust doth corrupt, and where thieves do not break through nor steal: for where your treasure is, there will your heart be also (Matt 6:19-21).

Jesus said your heart will follow your treasure. If all your treasure is here, your heart is here. But if you have some treasure stored in Heaven, you'll look forward to going because your heart will be there.

Rich and rebellious kings, merchants, and captains will mourn because their treasure is gone. They speculated and invested in Antichrist, and they lost it all in a single hour.

Babylon's Fall Celebrated (18:20-24)

Babylon's crash is mourned by those who are heavily invested in her. But not everybody mourns.

Heaven rejoices (18:20)

Rejoice over her, thou heaven, and ye holy apostles and prophets; for God hath avenged you on her (18:20).

What a difference! There's no funeral in Heaven. The saints prayed for it; the Old Testament prophets and New Testament apostles predicted it; and now they are all called to enjoy it. Righteousness has prevailed.

Babylon disappears (18:21-24)

And a mighty angel took up a stone like a great millstone, and cast it into the sea, saying, Thus with violence shall that great city Babylon be thrown down, and shall be found no more at all. And the voice of harpers, and musicians, and of pipers, and trumpeters, shall be heard no more at all in thee; and no craftsman, of whatsoever craft he be, shall be found any more in thee; and the sound of a millstone shall be heard no more at all in thee; and the light of a candle shall shine no more at all in thee; and the voice of the bridegroom and of the bride shall be heard no more at all in thee: for thy merchants were the great men of the earth; for by thy sorceries were all nations deceived. And in her was found the blood of prophets, and of saints, and of all that were slain upon the earth (18:21-24).

Jeremiah's instruction to Seraiah predicted the ultimate demise of Babylon. His words were twice prophetic, first for ancient Babylon and second for commercial Babylon, wherever it may be located.

And Jeremiah said to Seraiah, When thou comest to Babylon, and shalt see, and shalt read all these words; then shalt thou say, O Lord, thou hast spoken against this place, to cut it off, that none shall remain in it, neither man nor beast, but that it shall be desolate for ever. And it shall be, when thou hast made an end of reading this book, that thou shalt bind a stone to it, and cast it into the midst of Euphrates: and thou shalt say, Thus shall Babylon sink, and shall not rise from the evil that I will bring upon her: and they shall be weary (Jer 51:61-64).

Like a stone cast into water that splashes and then disappears, so will be the violent, sudden, and complete annihilation of Babylon, symbol of man's rebellion and power. Man is no more than a pipsqueak when it comes to God's power and judgment. Even the ripple on the water will disappear.

The city falls silent: no more music, factories, neon lights, family life, or social life. The power base of the Antichrist will be gone and his deception through Babylon unmasked. Antichrist is unveiled in Revelation as surely as Jesus Christ is.

The parallels between Babylon and Babel are obvious:
1. At Babel, man proposed world unity by common worship and tongue. God defeated it.
2. Religious Babylon proposes a world church. God destroys it through the beast.
3. Political Babylon tries world government and world common market. Christ destroys it.

Edward Gibbon gave five reasons Rome fell in *The Decline and Fall of the Roman Empire:*

    1. Undermining of the dignity and sanctity of the home, the basis for human society.
    2. Higher and higher taxes to provide free bread.
    3. The mad craze for pleasure, brutal and immoral.
    4. Building of great armaments when the enemy is within — decay of individual responsibility.
    5. The decay of religion — faith becomes form.

These will bring down Babylon — and the United States, if we continue to decline.

Man's best efforts go up in smoke!

What a dramatic end to the Great Tribulation. The best man can do is destroyed by Jesus Christ in one hour. When the sun sets, man's glory — and Satan's — lies in shambles.

That's the way it is in salvation, too. The best you can do is worth nothing in the sight of God and will only lead to destruction. You must come by the way of the cross and the Lord Jesus Christ, or you will be eternally lost.

Man's way — and Babylon's — is rebellion. God will not accept it. The end of man's way is always death.

When your life is a shambles, Jesus is just a prayer away. When man's best lies in ruins, the return of Jesus Christ in power and glory is just minutes or hours away. The stage is perfectly set for his dramatic entrance.

Immediately after the tribulation of those days shall the sun be darkened, and the moon shall not give her light, and the stars shall fall from heaven, and the powers of the heavens shall be shaken: and then shall appear the sign of the Son of man in heaven: and then shall all the tribes of the earth mourn, and they shall see the Son of man coming in the clouds of heaven with power and great glory (Matt 24:29-30).

Even so, come Lord Jesus!

Bibliography

Archer, Gleason L., Jr. "Daniel." In *The Expositor's Bible Commentary.* Vol 7. Ed. Frank E. Gaebelein. Grand Rapids: Zondervan Publishing House, 1985.

Bunyan, John. *The Pilgrim's Progress.* Carlisle, PA: The Banner of Truth Trust, 1977 rep. ed. [1895].

The Holy Bible. Scofield Reference edition. New York: Oxford University Press, 1945.

Johnson, Alan F. "Revelation." In *The Expositor's Bible Commentary.* Vol 12. Ed. Frank E. Gaebelein. Grand Rapids: Zondervan Publishing House, 1981.

McGee, J. Vernon. *Thru the Bible.* 5 vols. Nashville: Thomas Nelson Publishers, 1983.

Pentecost, J. Dwight. *Things to Come.* Grand Rapids: Zondervan Publishing House, 1958.

Peterson, Eugene H. *The Message.* Colorado Springs, Colorado: NavPress Publishing Group, 1994.

Thomas, Robert L. "2 Thessalonians." In *The Expositor's Bible Commentary.* Vol 11. Ed. Frank E. Gaebelein. Grand Rapids: Zondervan Publishing House, 1978.

Walvoord, John F. *Jesus Christ Our Lord.* Chicago: Moody Press, 1969.

________.*The Holy Spirit.* Grand Rapids: Zondervan Publishing House, 1958.

________.*The Return of the Lord.* Grand Rapids: Zondervan Publishing House, 1955.

________.*The Revelation of Jesus Christ.* Chicago: Moody Press, 1966.

Walvoord, John F., and Zuck, Roy B. *The Bible Knowledge Commentary.* 2 vols. Wheaton: Victor Books, 1983.

Young, Robert. *Analytical Concordance to the Bible.* Grand Rapids: William B. Eerdmans Publishing Company, 1970.